"Happy genius
of my household"

"Happy genius of my household"

A Son's Memoir of William Carlos Williams

WILLIAM ERIC WILLIAMS

EDITED BY IAN D. COPESTAKE

Foreword by Paul Mariani

McFarland & Company, Inc., Publishers
Jefferson, North Carolina

Library of Congress Cataloging-in-Publication Data

Names: Williams, William Eric, 1914–1995 author | Copestake, Ian D., 1969– editor
Title: "Happy genius of my household" : a son's memoir of William Carlos Williams / William Eric Williams ; edited by Ian D. Copestake.
Description: Jefferson, North Carolina : McFarland & Company, Inc, 2026 | Includes bibliographical references and index.
Identifiers: LCCN 2026033582 | ISBN 9781476699554 paperback ♾ ISBN 9798368601397 ebook
Subjects: LCSH: Williams, William Carlos, 1883–1963—Family | Williams, William Eric, 1914–1995—Family | Poets, American—20th century | BISAC: BIOGRAPHY & AUTOBIOGRAPHY / Personal Memoirs | LITERARY CRITICISM / Poetry | LCGFT: Biographies
Classification: LCC PS3545.I544 Z975 2026
LC record available at https://lccn.loc.gov/2026033582

ISBN (print) 978-1-4766-9955-4
ISBN (ebook) 979-8-3686-0139-7

Front cover images: William Carlos Williams, December 22, 1948, attic of 9 Ridge Road; *inset* William Eric Williams near Nadi, on Viti Levu, Fiji islands, 1943 (both photographs courtesy of the Poetry Collection of the University Libraries, University at Buffalo, The State University of New York).

Printed in the United States of America

McFarland & Company, Inc., Publishers
Box 611, Jefferson, North Carolina 28640
www.mcfarlandpub.com

To the memory of
Emily Mitchell Wallace
(1933–2019)

Acknowledgments

IAN D. COPESTAKE

All previously unpublished material by William Carlos Williams is quoted by permission of the estates of Dr. William Eric Williams and Dr. William Carlos Williams on behalf of Daphne Williams Fox, the executrix of both estates. General but grateful acknowledgment is given to New Directions Publishing Corporation for permission to quote from previously published writing by William Carlos Williams. Excerpts from THE COLLECTED POEMS OF WILLIAM CARLOS WILLIAMS, VOL. 1 by William Carlos Williams, copyright ©1938–1952 by William Carlos Williams, copyright ©1957–1974 by Florence H. Williams. Reprinted by permission of New Directions Publishing Corp. and Carcanet Press. Excerpts from THE COLLECTED POEMS OF WILLIAM CARLOS WILLIAMS, VOL. 2 by William Carlos Williams, copyright ©1944–1962 by William Carlos Williams, copyright ©1963 by the Estate of William Carlos Williams. Reprinted by permission of New Directions Publishing Corp. and Carcanet Press. Excerpts from THE AUTOBIOGRAPHY OF WILLIAM CARLOS WILLIAMS, by William Carlos Williams, copyright ©1951 by William Carlos Williams. Reprinted by permission of New Directions Publishing Corp. Introduction to YES, MRS. WILLIAMS: A PERSONAL RECORD OF MY MOTHER, copyright ©1982 by William Eric Williams. Reprinted by permission of New Directions Publishing Corp.

All previously published material from the *William Carlos Williams Newsletter* and *William Carlos Williams Review* appear with the permission of The Pennsylvania State University. Unpublished letters in the private collection of the Williams family quoted here (such as from Florence Herman Williams to William Carlos Williams and medical reference cards) are part of the Williams Family Archive.

Sincere thanks to Alison Fraser at the Poetry Collection of the University Libraries, University at Buffalo, The State University of New York. Thanks also to Emily Huff and family as well as to Laura Parr and her relatives for their patience and trust. A special word of thanks to Peggy Fox for her fantastic help in putting me on the right track and also to Jeehan Quijano for her heroic transcription efforts in preparing the manuscript.

Table of Contents

Table of Contents

Preface

Ian D. Copestake

William Carlos Williams begins his autobiography with a reflection that "[n]ine-tenths of our lives is well forgotten."[1] This also rings true in relation to the history of any publication, because from the point of view of an author or editor, no book's reader will ever know even a quarter of the story of how what they hold in their hand or read on a screen has finally come into being. Unless, that is, they are presented with a brief slice of its history, which is what I would like to do in the following.

Over the years William Eric Williams, the eldest son of William Carlos Williams, was asked to contribute prefaces to this and that publication or to write short articles about his father, who had become more well known and achieved greater recognition for his poetry after his death than had been the case for most of his life. As the previously unpublished 1981 interview with William Eric that concludes this memoir confirms, the eldest son continued to respond to and assist scholars writing about his father for decades after William Carlos Williams's death in 1963. He also confirms that his own publication of reflections on life with his poet-doctor father led to him being encouraged to add to them and so complete a memoir of his own. One such researcher who encouraged him was Emily Mitchell Wallace, who, along with Theodora (Teddy) Rapp Graham, had established early inroads into scholarship on Williams and his work through the publications that emerged from their respective PhD dissertations on the poet undertaken in the 1960s.[2] Through her own research subsequent to publishing the earliest bibliographic volume of Williams scholarship, Emily Mitchell Wallace was one of the many visiting scholars William Eric recalls hosting in his interview. But Emily also became close to the family and aided Florence (Flossie) Williams during the period of bereavement following the death of Flossie's husband.

By the early 1980s, William Eric thus had a collection of essays that various people including Emily, Teddy, and Peggy Fox (by then the president of New Directions publishing house, an institution so intrinsic to Williams's career) urged him to publish. Indeed, without the efforts of Peggy, above and beyond her 36 years working at New Directions, which she had joined in 1975, the current publication would not exist. Emily had thus connected William Eric with Harry Ford, the esteemed poetry editor at Knopf, and an agreement was reached to publish his essays and prefaces with additional sketches. But before a contract was drawn up, in 1995, William Eric died, and then, four years later, Harry Ford died, and so the project was "orphaned."

However, James Laughlin, famed founder of New Directions, was still alive at this point, and he said, "[w]ell, I suppose we should do it." And so, in the late nineties, contracts were drawn up by New Directions with William Eric's heirs, two of his daughters on the one hand and his widow Mimi (Mary Parr Williams) on the other. Mimi and Emily had an understanding that Emily would edit the project when she had time, but Emily didn't want a contract until she was ready to devote herself to it (Peggy suggests that New Directions did draw up a contract with her in 2007 or 2008). Regardless, Emily was working on the project from the late nineties, and Peggy even had Sylvia Frezzolini Severance (who had designed the beautiful New Directions editions of *The Selected Letters of Tennessee Williams*) work up a design for William Eric's book. At this point in the story, if you will allow me, euphemisms must be employed to ensure at the very least that the truth behind the Williams quote with which I began be honored! Suffice it to say, then, that delays arose and complications ensued, and no book appeared. With Peggy's retirement from New Directions in 2011, Emily's attempt to realize this project ran aground, as she had lost her key ally, and a new publisher would have to be found if the book was ever to see the light of day. This state of limbo sadly continued until Emily's own death in 2019.

Then, in the summer of 2020, a friend of Emily's, Margot Barringer, contacted Peggy to discuss the project and see about reviving it, driven now by the estate of both Emily and her late husband, Gregory

M. Harvey. The estate's representative, led by Emily Pace, in turn contacted me and I agreed to pick up the baton. My involvement thus began in April 2021. Files were recovered, permissions were gained, and a publisher was found. And the book, after a very long journey, is now in your hands.

So ends one story. But I would also like to add a personal note that is related to the above only by the fact that I was also one of the scholars who contacted William Eric Williams for help with my own research on his father's poetry and life. I was in the middle of my PhD studies on Williams's poetry and the specific influence of Unitarianism on his outlook and motivation; and from my digs in Leeds, England, I was somewhat at a loss as to how I could learn more about the local history of the association of William Eric's father with the Rutherford Unitarian Society (which William George, William Carlos's English father, had established) from so far away and with no likelihood of visiting in person. So I wrote directly to William Eric at the famed address (to Williams scholars, anyway!) of his medical practice on 9 Ridge Road and which he had taken over from his father. And I received a reply! But not just a reply: it was an envelope containing a photocopy William Eric had made of a document I had been seeking but had only one brief reference to and which I included in my letter to him, more out of hope than any expectation. But it had been enough and it had been duly dispatched, and it was eventually received as if I was a child again receiving an early morning Christmas present![3]

But what strikes me most now, even more than the fact that the envelope from Rutherford contained a neat, handwritten, ruled note on prescription pad notepaper headed with the lauded address of his practice, on which was written "[h]ope these are helpful to you. Lots of luck," is that the note is dated 5.17.95. William Eric was still helping scholars from around the world learn about his father's work a mere two months before his own death. I thus remain humbled and am happy to be able to end this particular story by playing a part in bringing William Eric's reflections to light in one place, not least because by doing so it allows me to record my own thanks for the generosity he showed me.

Foreword

Paul Mariani

Though I have immersed myself in teaching and writing about William Carlos Williams's life, poetry and prose for more than half a century now, and though I've published numerous essays and poems as well as two books on the man and his literary reputation—including *A New World Naked* back in 1981—reading William Eric Williams's memoir has only reinforced my love and admiration for both father and son.

The Williams connection began for me back in 1967, when I was completing my dissertation on Gerard Manley Hopkins and happened to spot a book called *Paterson* in a local bookstore near Queens College just outside Flushing, Long Island. At the time I was teaching undergrads at Hunter and cops (including Frank Serpico) at John Jay College, which was located down on 23rd Street in Manhattan back then. Paterson? I remember thinking. Who would write a book-length poem about Paterson, the place where my mother's Polish father was raised before he joined the U.S. Cavalry and where many of my Swedish relatives had worked in the silk mills in the early part of the twentieth century? As a boy of nine or ten I remember crawling under the steel fence with my younger brother Walter and looking down at the crash of the Passaic River as it loomed then rushed over the Great Falls with a power which still sends tremors through me.

I spent the first five years of the '70s researching all the information I could find on Williams between 1910 and the early 1970s for what would become my second book, *William Carlos Williams: The Poet and His Critics*, all by way of preparing a study of Williams's

Paterson. But no editor seemed interested in the story behind the epic, though one said he'd be interested in a biography of the Jersey doctor-poet.

And so began my research at Yale, Buffalo, Texas, Baltimore, and a dozen other places to gain enough material to present myself to Flossie Williams and ask for her permission and to get her blessing for the project. And so it was in the summer of 1976 that I introduced myself to Dr. William Eric Williams, who was out working in the garden of the Williams home at 9 Ridge Road in Rutherford, only to inform me that, yes, his mother was home—upstairs—but that she was now close to death. Still, he seemed interested in the project I had undertaken. And so began a long and close relationship with him and with his brother, Paul, who in time trusted me with a huge collection of letters and other materials written by their father to their mother.

And so the project continued, with me staying at the Williams household on several occasions, including one visit when I was accompanied by Adam Horvath, my editor at McGraw-Hill. The biography was of course a huge undertaking, note after note and page after page typed out on my wife's small typewriter and using hundreds of three-by-five index cards with information, along with hundreds of Xeroxed pages provided by a host of terrific librarians and their assistants. At one point I asked my chairman if I could spend a semester to complete the project and make up teaching classes later. When he refused, my wife Eileen and I cobbled our resources—she teaching kindergarten with three small boys at home—and I wrote day after day after day. When *A New World Naked* was finally published, it came to 900 pages.

Of course, as I was a professor at the University of Massachusetts teaching Modern Poetry, my primary interests focused on the intersection of the poet's life as a poet, with as much information as I could gather about Williams's life as a physician in the Rutherford area of New Jersey, with his specialty in obstetrics and pediatrics. Talks with Dr. Robert Coles helped me with that aspect in particular, as well as with Dr. William Eric. I interviewed Williams's patients and the nurses he worked with, and even the local druggist, who told me that Williams would hand a patient a note for a prescription, with a code written at the top which meant "I didn't charge this patient for the visit, because he didn't have the money," and the druggist would in turn give the patient the prescribed medicine without charging. How often does that happen today, one wonders? But that was William Carlos Williams, good doctor that he was.

And it is just here that William Eric Williams's memories of his father have resonated most deeply with me: how the eye of the physician helped shape the way William Carlos Williams came to see the world about him, using words to shape that world through a free-for-all modern imagination. Of course, there was Modernism, Dadaism, Vorticism, Surrealism, the shapeshifting images of Matisse, Picasso, Georgia O'Keefe, Marcel Duchamp, and his friends, Marsden Hartley and Charles Sheeler among them.

But at the heart of it all was Williams's trained eye of seeing what was there before him: the inscape (to use a term Manley Hopkins used, but which also helps explain Williams) of the present moment. The sense, that is, of seeing the new world naked, the way we all enter the world: that extraordinary moment as we experience a new life, as Williams witnessed again and again and again—having delivered more than 3,000 babies over his years as a doctor. The way, in the face of death and contagious disease, a country doctor driving along a New Jersey highway on a cold, early spring morning notices among the "waste of broad, muddy fields / brown with dried weeds, standing and fallen // patches of standing water" those first signs of life returning: that "reddish / purplish, forked, upstanding, twiggy / stuff of bushes."[1] Like a newborn, yes, and yes, like the words of a poem, which at first seem "Lifeless in appearance." And yet they—we—all "enter the new world naked, / cold, uncertain of all / save that they enter":

> One by one objects are defined—
> It quickens: clarity, outline of leaf
>
> But now the stark dignity of
> entrance—Still, the profound change
> has come upon them: rooted, they
> grip down and begin to awaken

Now. And again now. And there we have it. No final period to close the poem. Instead, like life itself re-emerging, the imagination continues on its way. One more spring unfolding in an endless cascade, the miracle of it all. Like those newborns entering a world and making us new again.

I remember going through those stacks of three-by-five cards

William Eric kept in a closet on the second floor of his home, cards his father had carefully written out with hundreds of facts, statistics, and summaries of each patient he saw over the years. And I remember talking with Robert Coles years ago, recalling his own time as a young intern, as he traveled with Bill Williams around Rutherford and environs as he made house calls, something doctors did in those long-gone days.[2] In particular, he remembers Williams talking in a doorway in Rutherford with an older woman in her bathrobe one wintry morning, checking up on her condition, and then returning to the car, remarking what a beautiful woman she was, where in truth Coles had thought the woman he'd just seen was just one more ordinary-looking patient. Or the time Williams paid a house call on an elderly widow living alone and how—noticing how cold the house was—had gone down into the basement to stoke the furnace and refill it with coal before leaving for his next house call. For what good was it leaving a patient in a cold house, he said, where she could easily get sick again? Multiply such acts a thousand times and more, and you get a sense of who this doctor was.

For me, William Eric's take on his mother Florence—Flossie—is especially revelatory in these pages. In the beginning, it was Charlotte, her older sister, who caught the young William Carlos's eye. But when she took a deeper interest in his brother, Edgar—the athletic, more dashing younger brother, who had already spent several years in Rome on a scholarship focusing on art and architectural design—Bill, after a fit of near-despair, began to turn his attention to Flossie, the younger, plainer sister, but the one who had a more solid sense of reality and would anchor her family over the next 50 years. After courting Flossie and becoming engaged to her, he left for Europe (again) and spent a year of postgraduate studies in Leipzig, Germany, studying pediatrics with some of the world's most advanced doctors. After his return home, the two married on December 12, 1912—12/12/12—and soon after settled into their Victorian home at 9 Ridge Road, Rutherford, just a few streets over from where he had been raised, and where he and Flossie would live their entire lives.

William Eric makes it clear that it was no secret to Flossie that Bill had an eye for women—as they had for him—and on a number of occasions she had to remind him that she was not blind to what might have happened or did happen between Williams and those women. Still, as the letters published here make clear, she turned a philosophical eye to his wanderings because she had a family to care for, a doctor's business to run (as she did smoothly) and most of all because she loved him—as he loved her—and knew his weaknesses.

But there were times too when they were in Paris in the mid–twenties (Williams's sabbatical year)—when Williams caught glimpses of a Dionysian side to Flossie, especially when she was out in gay Paree at a nightclub with her female friends. Which must have reminded him that there might well have been two sides to these impulses. But Flossie stayed anchored, bless her. As for Bill, how many times did he confess to her, both for his weaknesses and for his love for his wife. As for example, take the poem "This Is Just to Say," a note tacked to the icebox back in 1934. It's a short poem, 33 words total including the title.[3] But it says so much. The title sets the poem up, almost casually: a little confession about eating the chilled plums he finds in the icebox one morning, when Floss is away, having placed a note on the icebox about what she had prepared for his lunch.

But is the poem simply about eating those plums? Or is it about something far deeper: consuming that forbidden fruit we find in the Garden of Eden, with Adam confessing to Eve this time?[4] But the real fruit, I suspect, was his earlier one-night stand with the millionairess Nancy Cunard in her apartment when he and Flossie were visiting Rome. What he remembered especially about Nancy was how cold and sweet and matter-of-fact this modern woman could be. "Let's go to bed first," she said, "and then we'll talk afterwards." Words to that effect. And Williams confessing it now, in a note tacked to that other icebox.

Flossie was smart, read voraciously, and commented on her husband's work and defended it endlessly, as she defended her husband, because she *knew* him. Knew his intelligence, his constant giving of himself day and night for his patients, losing some to conditions beyond any doctor's control, but saving the vast majority of them. And then there was his incessant need to write poems and novels and short stories and plays and, yes, even, like Ezra Pound with his internationally-based *Cantos*, an American epic called *Paterson*, a poem constantly at odds with itself like his America, trying to settle on an "antagonistic cooperation" with itself.

And of course there is Williams's late poem "Asphodel, That Greeny Flower," a love letter to Flossie in his last years, after having suffered the insults of a heart attack and a series of strokes that damaged his right side and his ability to speak, as well as the insults heaped upon him as he was investigated by the FBI for what they saw as left-leaning tendencies, but were in reality his compassion for others here and abroad. And now, in the age of the atom bomb and death always imminent, with the time he knew he had left, he had to try and explain what sort of man he had been, and why Flossie, despite his short-lived affairs, had always been at the center for him. What carried us through was the imagination, the ability to see flowers even in Hell, the belief that love could outlive death.

> It was the love of love,
> the love that swallows up all else,
> a grateful love,
> a love of nature, of people,
> animals,
> a love engendering
> gentleness and goodness
> that moved me
> and *that* I saw in you.
> [...]
> My heart rouses
> thinking to bring you news
> of something
> that concerns you
> and concerns many men. Look at
> what passes for the new.
> [...]
> Hear me out
> for I too am concerned
> and every man
> who wants to die at peace in his bed
> besides.[5]

This was his confession: halting, starting over multiple times, stammering to make a full confession, even as he tried to explain that the sexual impulses he had felt were as old as the characters in the *Iliad*, Helen included. But my sense is that Flossie knew all this long before Williams, close now to death, composed his own aubade.

I remember William Eric telling me back some 40 years ago how he wished his father could have gone fishing with him and Paul, rather than go with one of the neighbors. But that was one of the sacrifices his father had to make to serve the Black community and the Italians of Guinea Hill and the German and Irish families spread out around Rutherford and environs, to say nothing of his time working in the local hospital. But now it is time to let William Eric Williams tell his family's story. I promise, it will touch you again and again.

Paul Mariani *is an award-winning poet; professor of English emeritus at Boston College; and biographer of William Carlos Williams, John Berryman, Robert Lowell, Hart Crane, and Gerard Manley Hopkins.*

"Happy genius of my household"

A Son's Memoir of William Carlos Williams

William Eric Williams

William Eric Williams, 1985. Photo by Mary (Mimi) Parr Williams. Williams family archive. Courtesy the Poetry Collection of the University Libraries, University at Buffalo, The State University of New York.

Author's Note: Closer to the Grain

A biography is an account of a person's life, usually a person of importance, someone who has made a mark in life which is of great significance. The account of such a life is a tribute to the famous person, a good story that will perhaps sell, a piece of history that should be recorded for future scholars, and finally a blueprint after which those sufficiently concerned may pattern their lives. The biographer who will construct this account may be an expert in the field in which the subject has gained fame, or a professional scholar-writer who will so research his subject that he or she will become such an expert. The reporting is for the most part retrospective, gleaned from documents and hearsay.

This reader has been impressed by the failure of most biographies to project an image of the subject; that is, his physical image and how he functions in the stream of everyday life. Perhaps I am looking for something that is not included in the definition of biography, but I think a more complete anatomical and physiological image would provide a sensory framework, a body of physical facts into which other facts of the biography could be inserted and thus perhaps more easily retained for future reference. Too often I come away from reading a biography with the feeling of having read a depersonalized account of a fictional character whom the author wouldn't recognize even if imprisoned with his hero in a cell on solitary row.

Like my father I am a medical doctor, and I propose to approach "biography" as I would a new "case." I elicit, as needed, the family history, the past history, the social history, the sexual history, and the occupational history. And finally, in medical cases, I propose the physical examination, with the laying on of hands, the palpation, auscultation, exploration of body orifices, measurement of temperature, pressure, heart rate; all of which in summation will yield a diagnosis. Does the patient have a legitimate somatic illness, or are we dealing with a psychosomatic problem, which, by the way, may prove to be a more devastating illness and tougher to "cure"?

This may be idiosyncratic whimsy on my part, precipitated initially by reading the biography of Pierre-Auguste Renoir written by his son, but having read four accounts of my father's life, I decided there was a part of him that was missing, because I knew the guy better than the scholars who were writing about him.[1] They understood and could interpret his art, but I had experienced the man in the flesh on a day-to-day basis and could perhaps fill gaps in the ego picture, that image somewhere between the id and superego that a man presents to the world around him. Will it be useful? Will it be relevant for those interpreting what he has created? What my father has written has never been of great significance to me, except for the prose stories of medical experiences and the biographical trilogy concerning my mother and her family.[2] I disqualify myself as a critic of his poetic art but will nevertheless quote from his poems.

It has been brought home to me forcibly by the letters I receive, by the media, and by the inquiring minds of children that my father is a man of importance to the art of poetry, apparently of greater significance now than in his lifetime, and his influence will undoubtedly continue in future years. Therefore I will rest easier in my grave knowing that it has been written that William Carlos Williams was a man who enjoyed lots of butter with his meals; rapped happily with the shop owners on Park Avenue (the main drag in Rutherford); took a tub bath once a week; and wore bow ties, conservative vests, and a fedora. The fact that he has always been a subject for disputation among scholars, and those who purport to be scholars, should not color the basic image of the man I remember, my father and my colleague as a doctor.

My sketches are episodes in the life of my Dad. The continuity results from the resonance of emotional memories. I paint his portrait through my observations; through the intimate, personal letters of family members; through reconstruction of the family and community environment in his formative years; and through extracts from his unusual diary consisting of a personal card file containing chronological entries of his notes at medical lectures and descriptions of plants and birds observed in his daily life. I have attempted to depict my father as an approachable "small-town boy" who would cause no turning of heads when encountered in a crowd, but who was admired and loved by many persons around the world, as well as in Rutherford and his New Jersey haunts.

Typically, in the presence of others, Dad was alert and friendly, a two-way conversationalist, willing to listen as well as speak his own opinion. In a group he was always involved, not one to drift into a corner, unless of course the subject failed to interest him, or the conversation was dominated by a dogmatic bore. At these times he was quite capable of excusing himself and walking out—or simply taking a catnap. In a mixed social gathering of neighborhood friends he was a catalyst. People were glad to see him. The men respected him for his fairness and slowness to judge, and knew he might laugh at their smutty stories. The women were titillated by his presence, their color rising a little when he addressed them, and were on occasion excited to bizarre acts of aggression, like the time a female friend of my parents (Louise Wagner) tried to comb his hair with a garden rake.

He had to develop strategies of escape and refusal. Yet there was nothing obtrusive in his manner. People seemed to sense that here was a nice guy who, far from being offended, welcomed human contact. How else to explain the little prostitute who grabbed his arm affectionately and asked, "[w]anna come home with me, Pop?" Mother, my younger brother Paul, Dad, and I were strung out somewhere between the old Astor and the Paramount on Broadway in Rutherford. Paul was escorting Mom up ahead, I was next in line, and Dad was sweeper. I heard her invitation and turned to see Dad smile and point up ahead with the remark, "I'm flattered, sweetheart, but maybe I'd better ask my wife." She too smiled, arched her eyebrows, and with a rather more philosophical moue veered off into the crowd.

Dad was, like Abou Ben Adhem, one who loved his fellow man, all except T.S. Eliot. To quote from Dad's *Autobiography*:

> Then out of the blue *The Dial* brought out *The Waste Land* and all our hilarity ended. It wiped out our world as if an atom bomb had been dropped upon it and our brave sallies into the unknown were turned to dust.
>
> To me especially it struck like a sardonic bullet. I felt at once that it had set me back twenty years, and I'm sure it did. Critically Eliot returned us to

> the classroom just at the moment when I felt that we were on the point of an escape to matters much closer to the essence of a new art form itself—rooted in the locality which should give it fruit.[3]

The deep impression made on me by Dad's admiration of and affection for Ezra Pound, Charles Demuth, Marsden Hartley, Stuart Davis, H.D., Marianne Moore, Charles Sheeler, Wallace Stevens, Wallace Gould, and other poets and painters, contrasted with his intense dislike of Eliot, was that the role of the poet mattered to him greatly, even though the proportion of his time and energy spent on poetry could be only a fraction of the time and energy required by his other roles. He devoted himself with passion and tenderness to the latter—grandson of Emily Dickinson Williams Wellcome; son of Raquel Hélène Rose Hoheb and William George; brother of Edgar Irving and uncle to Ed's daughters, Palamona, Ingrid, Edith, and Christina; husband of Florence Hilda Herman; grandfather of my four daughters, Emily, Erica, Elaine, and Daphne, and of my brother Paul's two children, Paul Jr. and Suzanne; an attentive physician to several thousand mothers and children, loyal citizen of the Borough of Rutherford, New Jersey, and of the United States of America, and a leading member of the international avant-garde.

My desire is to capture the essence of the man, to mold the image so it will fit him as the shell of the nut cradles the meat. All the world's a stage, and every man through his motions and emotions, conscious or unconscious, creates a canvas that may give him immortality. Charlie Chaplin waddling west into the sunset, his feet shuttling rapidly to north and south. The nymphs of Edgar Degas. The nudes of Renoir. The crass clowning of Jimmy Durante. The subtle nuances of Jack Benny. The left hook of Joe Louis. The legerdemain of Harry Houdini. Each in his own right an artist, and easily distinguishable by his inimitable hallmark. Make it simple, like the logician favoring the least complicated hypothesis to support the solution to the problem. That is my aim.

In our daily life together as a family, my brother Paul and I always shared a little act, pantomiming a characteristic, visible state of mind of Dad's. It consisted of complete detachment from reality as we knew it, with eyes unfocused, gait automatic, all receptors turned off. The musical accompaniment was a tuneless whistling evoked by tootling the gently exhaled breath between tongue and hard palate. This we aped, but still respected, as an indicator that something profound was taking place. As far as we knew he was never aware of what was happening behind his back. You might say he was on his cloud nine. Poet busy creating.

William Eric Williams, M.D.
9 Ridge Road, Rutherford, New Jersey
1995

1

In the Beginning

William Carlos Williams was born on September 17, 1883, in Rutherford, New Jersey. Both his parents had grown up in the West Indies, his mother retaining French citizenship, and his father remaining an English citizen all his life. Rutherford was a small town which had just two years previously been incorporated as a Borough. The population was less than 2,000.

The first Rutherford Borough Ordinance passed in December 1881 stated "[t]hat no person shall drive over or upon the sidewalks of any street or any highway in said Borough, any horse, vehicles, cow, goat, sheep or other animals."[1] This allegedly resulted from the townspeople's irritation at "playing hopscotch with animal droppings every time they walked down the [wood] sidewalks."

It was a rural environment although within sight of the New York city skyline. My father's eardrums would vibrate to the sounds of the cock's crow in the morning; the moo of the cow at milking time; the grating of iron-bound wagon wheels on gravel at his front door; the huffing crescendo of the coal-burning engines, double-hitched, coming up the slight slope from Secaucus to the Bergen cut-off; the clanging of the Presbyterian Church bell that sounded the alarm for fire. No sirens; no screaming airplanes overhead; no automobiles and their rattles, squealing tires and blatant horns, no telephone; no TV or radio, no sudden glare of light at the touch of a switch.

Within the house itself, a muted and harmonious phonic milieu, he heard his mother's piano and his father's flute; the pump moving water from the cistern to the attic reservoir; the stoking of a wood stove and the rattling of the burner lids and hot water tank cover; the background speech of Spanish; the opening and closing of screen doors on trips to the outdoor toilet; and in seasons with the windows open, the sounds of birds which later in life would so intrigue him: sparrows, robins, bluebirds, jays, warblers in profusion, cardinals, mockers, crossbills, and thrushes. At night the owls and whippoorwills, and the nighthawks far overhead in the evening giving their harsh "seep" cry. Day ended with the setting of the sun. There were no streetlights the first few years of his life.

The house, then unnumbered, now 131 West Passaic Avenue, was large, square, high-ceilinged, centrally placed on a large lot with a deep back yard. As a tot of three, many years later, I found it roomy and gloomy when placed there for a week to avoid confusion at 9 Ridge Road due to the approaching delivery of my brother Paul. I counted the steep back stairs many times in Spanish when Nana took me up to bed—*uno, dos, tres,* etc., up to *diez.* They converged in the central upstairs corridor with the shallower two-tiered front staircase. In this Victorian environment, with heavy drapes between rooms, central overhead chandeliers with beaded skirts, tall bookcases with glass doors, many photographs, a shallow living room fireplace, the baby "Willie" would grow without competition for a year preceding his brother Edgar's birth. Until he was six or seven he experienced the sight and odor of paint brushes and pigments used by his mother to create small floral and still-life groups before she discarded her paints and brushes in the attic to be found and used a decade later by her teenaged sons.

His father, William George, in the background was less an everyday influence as he played with his stamp collection, composed largely of the stamps of Central and South America, the West Indies, and British colonies. These were the countries where he traveled, and with the local druggists with which he would correspond in the course of business. Hundreds of stamps, meticulously cleaned, were mounted with great precision in notebooks and catalogues, the price penciled in beneath each. Apparently, he had a market for his philatelic material. His impression on the baby would come more from his shop in the back yard, the sounds of hammer, plane, and saw with which he was an able journeyman. Evenings as the infant dozed off, there was at times the sound of his father's voice reading the classics to his wife by lamplight. When his parents played music together, or when Uncle Irving hit a big drum, Baby Willie, hardly a year old, demonstrated perfect timing and appreciation of the rhythmic beat of an established pattern with his contribution on a little drum.[2]

A grape arbor led straightaway from the back porch, dividing the yard roughly into halves. To the left, lawn and a flower border. To the right, a vegetable patch. A nicely maintained area of greenery to condition an infant's eye. Dandelions, violets, lilacs, narcissi, daisies, roses, crocus, Queen Anne's Lace, each in its season will impress its pattern and color into the developing brain. Here too his introduction to the elements, wind and rain, gray cloud and bright sun, and how each modified the garden of blooms, their emergence in spring and fruition in summer, the harvest of fall and the cold blanket of winter. These primeval experiences will live with him always. Describing his walks with his close schoolboy friend Jim Hyslop, he would write many years later, "just to know the flowers was all I wanted."[3]

On landing at Le Havre, age 13, his most lasting impression was of a girl with a basket of violets singing "*Voilà d'jolies violettes!*"[4] At the school in Geneva, on climbing the Saleve he was startled by "the ground covered with blue gentians between the maplike snow patches."[5] On the school grounds, "I first became acquainted with the native yellow primrose, so delightfully sweet scented."[6]

Some years later, specifically May 8, 1908, Dad noted in his card index concerning the yard at 131 West Passaic, in his card index, "[n]o definite class of data to be collected. The plan to be general." "Quince blossoms just little, beautiful, pink peaks with wide spreading green corola below." And further on, "Mulberry tree not yet in full leaf. Certainly a dainty, light tree. Reminds me of Botticelli."

There is a six-card record from April 28 to June 1, 1908, detailing his observations of the dandelion crop on the property. In removing all the plants from the back lawn he notes that there were two distinct varieties, and goes into detail about their foliage and flower structures. He finds the roots extend down ten inches or less into the earth, and they are infested with a white wingless aphid, which is chaperoned by a bright yellow ant who consumes "[t]he pure crystal excrescence seen on caudal extrem. of aphis." Ten days later on a walk following three days of rain, "[a] field containing many beautifully developed specimens gave off a most delightful and peculiar odor, which for a time I was at a loss to trace to its origin, but at length found that it came from dandelions."

The influence of all these basic stimuli will recur in his poetry years later. The colors of flowers experienced the world over:

"Happy genius of my household"

from THE DISPUTANTS (1921)

Upon the table in their bowl
in violent disarray
of yellow sprays, green spikes
of leaves, red pointed petals
and curled heads of blue[7]

The rhythmic tattoo of the drum:

from THE DANCE (1944)

In Brueghel's great picture, The Kermess,
the dancers go round, they go round and
around [...][8]

The yard full of flowers:

from THE FLOWER (1930)

A flower, at its heart (the stamens, pistil,
etc.) is a naked woman [...][9]

His father's love of order and symmetry:

BREAKFAST (1938)

Twenty sparrows
on

a scattered
turd:

Share and share
alike.[10]

The character of an individual tree:

from YOUNG SYCAMORE (1927)

eccentric knotted
twigs
bending forward
hornlike at the top[11]

1. In the Beginning

The perfume of dandelions and primrose:

from SMELL! (1917)

Oh strong-ridged and deeply hollowed
nose of mine! what will you not be smelling?[12]

And his "Mulberry tree not yet in full leaf" and "Botticelli":

from THE BOTTICELLIAN TREES (1930)

The alphabet of
the trees

is fading in the
song of the leaves[13]

2

The House

The house at 9 Ridge Road was a gift from Pa Herman. His wedding present of $2,000 provided the down payment.[1] He held the $6,000 mortgage for the balance, and semi-annually Mom and Dad made payments to him of 5 percent interest. In turn he made semi-annual gifts of these amounts to Mom at Christmas and on her birthday. The property was left to them in his will. It's a sizable frame structure, clapboard finish, which had a gingerbready front porch that was removed in the 1920s. Two red brick chimneys on the south and east sides served the two furnaces and the fireplace in the living room. The structure stands on the south boundary line of the lot, with ample front, back and, north side yards. Over the years its color has been predominantly a light mustard shade. Six feet above the street level on a terraced plane, it has been a buttress against the advance of commercial progress into our neighborhood. The front door opens to the west, where the 102 bus from Hackensack to Newark guns its motors for the climb up Ridge Road, and where until the twenties trolley cars made a similar run over the tracks in the middle of the red brick paved Park Avenue. The family have never used this entrance much. The back door opens to the east in an angle formed by the meeting of the house and office walls. It catches the first rays of sun in the morning, and the five wooden steps descending to the yard have over the years been our late winter and early spring bleachers for sunbathing and backyard bloom surveillance. This has always been the family entrance. From the bottom of the stairs a 30-foot walk of flat field stones leads straight ahead to the garage. No masterpiece of masonry, but a labor of love for which Dad hauled the rocks from hither and yon over a period of several years.

Through the back door, one enters a small hallway. To the right and down two steps is the office. Straight ahead was the old icebox, whence came the ice-cold plums of the poem.[2] To the left is the door to the kitchen. Across the kitchen and through a swinging door is the dining room, a square chamber, relieved on the east wall by an alcove containing the sideboard. Above it hangs an Audubon print, *The Great Blue Heron*. Dad rescued the picture in pieces from the garret of a friend, and Mom found an understanding old German picture framer who restored it to its present condition. She vividly recalls unwrapping the tattered old print in his New York shop, and his exclaiming, "Ach, mein Gott, ein genuine Audubon; sure I fix 'im for you." In the center of the room is the Stickley oak dining table "made in Ohio," the matching black leather-seated chairs standing around the walls. Suspended dead center from the ceiling was a six-sided, rose-glass-paned chandelier, with a six-inch skirt of strings of rose-colored beads hanging within two feet of the tabletop. On occasion, when Dad attacked the far side of the roast, arm and chandelier would collide, bringing down a shower of beads that bounced indiscriminately into sugar bowl, fruit salad and mashed potatoes. Dad always sat facing the two windows in the south wall, with Mom to his left, me to the right, and my brother directly opposite. Dad's back was toward the front hall, whence the telephone could be brought on its extension cord and placed at his right elbow for convenience at mealtimes. Thus, the mood, pace and flavor of our meals was often determined by conversations with the hospital or sick patients—i.e. rupture of membrane, frequency of contraction, and rectal findings in delivery cases; or frequency, amount, consistency and color of vomitus and stools in gastro-enteritis. Also to his right, the early American corner cupboard, with a brick-colored earthenware Mexican jug on the top. In the early twenties Charlie Demuth gave the folks one of his delicate floral watercolors, *Pink Lady Slippers*, in appreciation for food, lodging, and medical care in the early stages of his diabetes.[3] They later bought *Tuberoses*, and the two hang there in the dining room to this day, rubbing elbows with works of Hank Niese, Harriet Gratwick, and Eyvind Earle (Mom's nephew).

Continuing clockwise to the right through double sliding doors is the wasp-waisted living room, a 30-foot expanse created by joining the old front and back parlors. Straight ahead to the west are five windows through which over the years we have watched the changing commercial scene along Park Avenue. Far up the block to the left is the Public Library, and in succession coming closer were Wahler's Candy Store, the

Presbyterian Parish House, Sing Lee's Laundry, Bobby Stuart's optometry office, Park Hardware, a First National Store, Park Cleaners, Davenport Drug, Korwan's Jewelry, Probst's Butcher Shop, the Mayflower Bakery, Benowitz Hardware, Handler's Bakery, Borschnecks' Flower Shop, Zimmerman's Haberdashery, and finally the old city hall containing the police station and post office. They have provided a characterless stretch of commercial fronts with an equally unexciting row of second floor apartments above them.

On the south wall is the red brick fireplace, Mom's desk on one side and a hand wound Victrola on the other. For perhaps the past 25 years, the fireplace has been handsomely sandwiched between ceiling-high bookcases, with breast-high cupboards beneath. An austere Charles Sheeler watercolor of tulips hangs dead center on the chimney. Here there was once a chin-high mantle, with a centrally placed glass-enclosed 30-day clock. At Christmas we kids hung our stockings there, beneath the decor of holly, ground pine, and cones, with miniature reindeer and woodcarvings of peasant figures peeping through. This wall served as the backdrop for Sheeler's wedding to Musya Sokolova, with a "piece-of-the-justice" (to quote Musya's misquotation of "justice of the peace") officiating. Here too Mom and Dad often sat on a two-sectioned couch, doing a crossword puzzle, reviewing correspondence, or reading. In front of them sat the copper-bound sea chest brought from China by Captain Ruud years ago and given to Dad apparently just because he liked him.[4] The north wall for years was dominated by a grand piano, and the intervening floor space has seen a parade of couches, tables, chairs, and rugs in styles from horsehair and wicker through Windsor spindles to modern sectionals. Around the remaining walls is a mélange of paintings, the majority of which are watercolors done by Dad's brother Edgar. Some have been there so long they spell a large part of my definition of home. A handsome portrait in oil of a golden-haired young woman was done by Dad's mother, Raquel Hélène Hoheb. Charlie Demuth's *End of the Parade—Coatesville, Pa.*[5] has a wall to itself, as does Marsden Hartley's pastel of what Dad was wont to refer to as Marsden's "breasts" (*Mountains in New Mexico*).

Through the living room and again exit clockwise to the right is the front hall. This completes the pattern of the ground floor. A strictly utilitarian room—coat closet, telephone stand, and chair, a large blanket chest built by Dad's good friend Russell Robinson during the Depression. Over the telephone stand is a big and fascinating print of Brueghel's *Children's Games.*[6]

To the right above the light switch hangs a copy of Ben Shahn's *Paterson,* done by the artist very informally and quickly at Roosevelt while Mom and Dad looked on. The left or north wall consists of the front door and the stairway to the second floor. A six-by-12-foot mural covers the wall back of the landing half way up the stairs. It is a scene by Eyvind Earle, looking down York Avenue on the east side of Manhattan from the 23rd floor of the Cornell Medical Center.[7] Included is the East River, with Turtle Bay in the background beneath the span of the 57th Street Bridge.

From the landing one bears right up the last seven steps to the second floor. It is a duplicate of the ground floor. A large central hall, with built-in linen closet and drawers straight ahead. Overhead center the light cord. On the left wall a bookcase jammed with books, and the top littered with family pictures and assorted memorabilia. Framing the linen closet are two bedrooms, the one to the left the nursery when we boys were kids, that to the right Mom and Dad's. Continuing right on the west wall another bedroom and full right coming north a short passage out to the sleeping porch, later enclosed to become Dad's mother's room. Against the rail that guards the stairwell in this upper hall stood her sewing machine, from whose drawers Smokey the cat would steal a spool of thread in the dead of night. While the house slept she wove her maze of thread around, over and under the downstairs furnishings to catch our feet and challenge our imaginations in the morning.

The door frame leading left into the passage to the bathroom contained a chinning bar when we boys were tads. Dad was concerned about our physical fitness, and the three of us did our daily dozen chins, with a few "skin-the-cats" and "skim-the-milks" thrown in. It was installed about five feet eight inches from the floor, which was high enough for us boys to need a stool to reach it, but just low enough so that Dad's brow met it squarely on a trip to the bathroom in the dark. I distinctly recall his vehement "Jesus Christ" startling me from my sleep on more than one occasion when someone had forgotten to take it down. In later years, when Paul and I were teenagers and staying out nights, that upper hall was the final obstacle to our getting to bed undetected. I won't say invariably, but I'll bet nine out of ten times the sneak from the head of

(From left) William Eric Williams, William Carlos Williams, and Paul Williams, 1926. Courtesy the Poetry Collection of the University Libraries, University at Buffalo, The State University of New York.

the stairs to our bedroom doors was interrupted by Dad's voice from his bed—"Did you have a good time?"

Capping it all is an undivided attic full of steamer trunks, furniture, pictures, chests of old clothing, and the assorted bric-a-brac and impedimenta of a small army of ancestors now dead, and of friends who have left things in trust and never returned. The family has never moved, so the attic contents have never had to be drastically reduced. It was a big barn of a place, unheated, without insulation and drafty in winter. A large gym mat once occupied the center of the floor, and there was a medicine ball, boxing gloves, and a punching bag. In the twenties Dad stapled sheets of insulation between the rafters, then closed off the space under the eaves and created an eight-foot ceiling with sheets of beaver board. It became his studio, with the desk, typewriter, file, and general literary storage area at the east end. On the wall at the opposite end, framing the window to the west, were two life-sized full-length caricatures, "La Mère Prudente" and "Le Pere Tranquil," done in watercolor by Dad's brother Edgar. The 35-foot north and south walls are plastered to this day with cartoons, posters, photos, children's drawings, primitive paintings, letters, postcards, and menus. The south wall features a four-foot graph of the course of the New York Stock Exchange from 1928 to 1932. Alongside, with what intent let the reader decide, is pasted a tiny clipping from an unknown periodical. It reads:

> I'm just a little prairie flower
> Growing wilder hour by hour
> Nobody even cultivates me
> I'm wild.

In the center of this wall is a chest-high shelf, six-feet long and slightly inclined like the old school desks, where he could stand and write. I recall his discussing the desirability of having facilities for writing in different bodily attitudes (sitting, reclining, standing), because the changes gave refreshment.

The heavy, black-stained wooden typing desk with the hinged foldaway top holding the typewriter is the central feature of the east end of the room. For ten years he worked here, with a coal stove in winter to make the temperature bearable, and fans in summer to temper the heat. An extension line was run up there and a phone installed. The light is a pull-cord overhead lamp, the flooring the original unfinished boards without carpeting. He sat on an adjustable, backless, screw-type stool while typing, and was a two-fingered, hunt-and-punch typist to his dying day. The sound of his typing when I was a youngster always gave me the impression that he was beating hell out of the machine. And this impression was fortified (on days when things didn't go right) by the scream of the roller as page after page was torn out, balled up, and pitched in the general direction of the wastebasket. Sometimes complete frustration drove him out into the yard to lose himself in sweaty garden labor for a couple of hours.

And it all sits on a full-sized, unfinished cellar, where the cat stepped delicately "first the right / forefoot / carefully" into the flowerpot on top of the jam closet.[8] But for us who lived here it was important as the focus of the coal-furnace-heat cycle. Winter mornings began between 6 and 7 a.m. when Dad went down to shake the furnace. The rattling of the iron grates in the furnaces was transmitted throughout the house. This was followed shortly by the sound of the coal shovel dug into the coal bin, and the chunks of anthracite tossed onto the residual hot coals from the previous day's fires. It was a daily ritual and our unofficial reveille. After school, Paul and I were responsible for hauling the ashes from the pits out to the garbage cans. The cycle was completed by the coal truck that made monthly deliveries, running a steel chute through the cellar window into the coal bins beneath the dining room. The truck bed was tilted upward and the coal rattled and roared down the chute, making conversation impossible when delivery was made at mealtime.

3

"Her Royal Highness"

From the beginning, of course, there was his mother, Raquel Hélène Rose Hoheb, a dynamic presence all of his life, even after her death at the age of slightly more than 102 years of age.[1] Born on December 24, 1847, in Mayagüez, Puerto Rico, she died in Rutherford in 1949 soon after her birthday. As her mother-in-law Emily Dickinson Wellcome had done before her, she had subtracted ten years from her age on official documents like census reports, and it was only after she died, when her poet son went to Puerto Rico and was shown her birth date in the "*big book of the Recorder in the Mayor's office*" in Mayagüez, that her true age was known.[2]

On reading Dad's *Yes, Mrs. Williams* a second time, I am left with a tremendous curiosity about its reason for being—about the importance of this obscure little woman, this product of a tropical hotbed on a West Indian island, this multinational mongrel gentlewoman transplanted to a northern, temperate zone suburb of a major metropolis infested with WASPs (as we now call white Anglo-Saxon Protestants). These entrepreneurs cared not a centime for her religious, social, or cultural background. How does this multilingual Francophile *señora* married to an Anglophile traveling-man citizen of Great Britain rate a book about herself? Examining the shreds of physical evidence that have come down to us, I find it abundantly apparent that her menfolk cared. Her older son Willie, writing from Philadelphia where he was a medical student, obviously cared. Witness the beginning of a long letter, composed in 318 Joseph Leidy, a room in the University of Pennsylvania Dormitories in West Philadelphia:

Sunday, Feb. 7, 1904

Dear Mama,

Today I spent part of the afternoon at Uncle's [Irving Wellcome's]. He had a big pile of old photographs which he had just taken out of a trunk and I was looking them over. As I was glancing from one picture to another I came upon a young girl of about twenty leaning on some old book. She was a beauty in fact she was such a girl as I have often dreamed of but never seen. I fell in love right away. She was not only beautiful for anyone could read her fine character through and through by looking into her eyes. She is as near my ideal as I have ever gotten. Mamy it was you. Now I can realize the popularity that must have been yours. I can see you flying across the ballroom floor in Paris with music softly playing and swaying dancers on every side. Oh it must have been great. That little picture has made me fall in you all over again. How coarse all the girls I know seem beside you [...].

Raquel Hélène Rose Hoheb, circa 1866–1877. Courtesy the Poetry Collection of the University Libraries, University at Buffalo, The State University of New York.

Love to you to Papa and to Ed.

Your son,

Willie

As a postgraduate medical student in Leipzig in 1909 he made a sentimental journey to Grimma "to see the remains of the nunnery where Katharina von Bora, Luther's bride, once lived."[3] This outing produced a letter to his mother enclosing a love poem to her, crafted in an old-fashioned meter and diction, though her name Elena or Hélène has been Americanized to Ellen:

3. "Her Royal Highness"

To Ellen Whom He Is Freeing

Thou priceless nun of a holy mind
Ellen lady of praise and song
Break from thy sleep in the darkness kind!
For me are the iron bars not strong.

Lady of anguish awake, awake
Thou princess of patience my lovely saint
Hark! tis the key which was forged to shake
Iron and stone to the last restraint.

What wrack is toil when the heart is free?
What loss is purity which has fled
To the hidden nest in the holy tree,
To the bubbling sand in the cold well's bed?

Oh what is age and what is time?
Tis always spring in the green heart's pale.
Love calls thee, awake! To the breech I climb.
Awake! In the forest I'll end my tale!

In the same week in Leipzig, in Dr. Curschmann's clinic, the subject of enteroptosis came up. As recorded in his notes: "Case. 1. A woman complains of pain in stom." Examination reveals a marbled belly due to application of poultices for relief pain. "A hollow epigastrium bet. navel and zyph. Epigastric pulsating. A decided prominence in region of navel and below. Pulsations may be: 1. Aorta. 2. Liver pushed by an enlarged hr. 3. True liver pulsation in 3 cuspid regurgitation. To left of linea alba the aorta is plainly felt." This was clinical jargon for a woman with a marked constriction at a point below the rib cage caused by corset pressure. So there was a rude jerking back to reality after the sentimental interlude at Grimma. And yet, in a way, a bit of comic relief. Fully revealed are the extremes of his poetic, philosophical, romantic imagination contrasted with the no nonsense vocabulary of medical doctors carefully observing a physical condition caused by the silly and harmful fashion of wearing tightly laced corsets. His poetic mother, of tiny waist, never needed a corset, nor did his wife.

She was my Nana Williams. She was small, gentle, and pleasantly scented. There was about her an aroma of Florida Water, lilac powder, and if lace and silk exude an essence, that must have been the other element that completed the bouquet. She carried herself as tall as her five feet and an odd inch or two would permit, her back very straight, the neck and chin rigidly squared by the whale-bone-supported lace collar and dickey that she habitually affected. Her speech was staccato, her language often punctuated with Spanish exclamations and French adages, for example, *"Pas de correspondence pour La Bastille,"* and *"Petit à petit l'oiseau fair son nid." "Madre de Dios," "Ai, Toledo!,"* and other Spanish expletives rattled off in what I am told was perfect Castilian, the "R"s particularly impressing me, the crescendo and decrescendo like summer thunder. When I was born, she was already approaching 70. Soon her husband would die—I recall a sick man in the room over the kitchen at 131 West Passaic Avenue, at the head of the back stairs, but I scarcely remember my grandfather. She was already showing the degenerative changes of old age—the rattling dental plates, the lateral deviation of her fingers at the metacarpopharlangeal joints, the early opacities of the optic lenses. The sense of failure, inadequacy, and the mental depression of early senility was upon her and inspired a letter of advice and encouragement, again from her son, Willie, addressed to Mrs. W.G. Williams, 2 Crescent Street, Newton Lower Falls, Massachusetts, where she was vacationing:

October 26, 1915

Dearest Old Silly Mommy,

Of course you're a failure—what good would you be if you didn't think yourself a failure? It's the fineness of your appreciations alone that makes you discontented with yourself. You are—you exist, you feel, you aspire, you love and you hate—the deep inexplicable burning in your innermost heart is real—it isn't a sham—it isn't false—therefore how can you really dare to tell me you are a failure? Of course you wish you had painted great pictures—you wish you had followed your voice—you wish you had married differently—yes you do, at times—you wish for self-confidence, happiness, pleasure—and when you have these last things you can't enjoy them.

In spite of everything you cannot free yourself—you fail to soar up into the sort of being you wish to be—therefore you call yourself a failure.

Mother dear—I also wish to do great works of art—to write great good poems—to help the poor and the unhappy—but young as I am who shall say that I will not be a failure?

Mother, that does not bother me in the slightest degree—it never has. I want to succeed of course but—so long as I can live a passionate life—full of striving, full of eager attempts to the whole extent of the power that is in me I shall say that I have really lived—that I have been really worthy of you—yes of you for you are to me perfect—say what you please—I cannot explain it.

Dear Mother, you are perhaps my dearest possession. Life is to be lived, Mother, not to be eaten.

Be good now and come home to me soon.

Your son that loves you dearly,

Willie

And in 1916 in response to a letter from his mother in which she defines "the three kinds of love," he would reply, "it is the first kind, the primitive, the furious kind that [Ezra] Pound shows most strongly—and that I show the least, by the way. It is that mysterious, mystic attraction of one person for another that Pound celebrates best." And here in the margin in pencil his mother inserts, referring to the "mystic attraction for another," "I too." Further along in his concluding paragraph he says, "[i]n our family the daring love of passion seems never quite to open its petals." And Momma again in pencil inserts, "but has exist." The very first woman in his life, the one from whose tissues he had issued, still waves her wand!

Her husband, William George Williams, being an Englishman, was a gardener, and the yard at 131 Passaic, aside from the annual vegetable patch, contained a grape arbor, cherry trees, quince, and apple trees. I can recall being led to the west fence line in the back yard where there was a low vine of a tiny grape variety, just the right for a toddler of my size. The fruits were pale lavender and very sweet. I like to think it was all planted with Raquel Hélène in mind, knowing her love of fruits, and providing material evidence of his concern for her comfort when he was away on frequent, extended business trips.

His letters also express his concern for her. Aboard the Hamburg-America liner *Atlas*, Pop Williams wrote to son Will, an intern at the old French Hospital in New York, while en route to Panama, stopping at Inagua in the Bahama Islands, and Kingston, Jamaica, among other ports:

1st Oct., 1907

Dear Will:

Up north and off Cape Hatteras, we were a bit shaken up; since then all is serene and fair.

I was not a moment sea-sick. Fare is good and I enjoy my meals.
The sea air is delightful....
While I am away, should be a good time for Mamma to get a little change and rest. Keep an eye on her. She wants care. [...] I want her to have a change from the housekeeping routine. [...] Take Mamma to museums, both of them, several times and take in a Sunday night opera concert. [...] Arrange it this way. Let Mamma run down [to New York] after church and take her out to lunch. Then visit the museum, take supper, and go to the concert returning home with her and sleep home, going down on Monday morning [to New York City]. Expense about $4.00 which she must charge to the housekeeping account. [...] And furthermore if you think she should have a greater change and rest, consider seriously the matter of three or four weeks at Jackson Sanatorium [...].

Love and a hug,

Pop

It was on the Connecticut shore of Long Island that HRH (the initials both for Her Royal Highness and Hélène Rose Hoheb) held summer court. There in the little frame cottage, she spent the hot months surrounded by the men of the Williams, Hoheb, and Wellcome clans, plus the gentlemen callers from the immediate neighborhood, like Professor Whelan of the Yale faculty (paleontology or geology) who had a cottage next door.

And then there was Mr. Hungerford, who of a summer evening would don his best bib and tucker, topped by a natty old Panama hat, and stroll down the oyster-shell drive from his home on the hill on the other side of Ocean Avenue. As his cane led the way around the corner of the front porch where Nana sat to watch the sunset over Woodmont Point, these two old friends would go into their act:

"Good evening, Mrs. Williams."
"Good evening, Mr. Hungerford."
"May I join you, Mrs. Williams?"
"Please. come and sit, Mr. Hungerford."

He with his Yankee twang, she with her correct but "francoise" English, exchanged the ancient amenities—posing, praising, parrying—quite content to be in each other's presence.

While across the lawn at their feet, and over the roughly piled fieldstone seawall, we are gathered around the fire on the beach above the high water line: Bill Wellcome, the musician, playing his ukulele and singing, Albert Hoheb, the physician son of Hélène's brother Carlos, and I, the son of Will, and about us the neighborhood gang that always assembles around a beach fire. We are the spawn of the Caribbean, couched here on another arm of the same great ocean. The same salt water as on the shores of Puerto Rico, Santo Domingo, and Martinique combs the eelgrass and winnows the sand on this shore. And above us in the shadows she sits and listens—the central thread, the tough core, this female totem.

Raquel's only rival was Flossie. During the years of World War I an already existing rivalry between Floss and Mamma was intensified. Because of Floss's father's ancestry, the local citizens had turned against him, and in fact a local vigilante group was staking out his home supposedly to monitor the place for subversive activities. Pa Herman was a German immigrant, a successful printer with his own shop in New York City. He had left Germany because of the saber rattling of Kaiser Wilhelm and had become a model of propriety, a church deacon, and, incidentally, the financier of the home Floss and Dad were occupying. This attitude of the vigilantes infuriated my father and he pointedly went to a neighboring German community, Carlstadt, and joined their *Turnverein* in protest. His mother was in turn infuriated, citing his French and English and Spanish ancestry as reason for condemning *Les Boche.*

Floss's family moved permanently from Rutherford to their farm in Munroe, New York, where they had spent their summers for years, but the hate rivalry endured for the rest of Nana Williams's life. Following a hip fracture, she was a dramatic presence for many years at 9 Ridge Road, getting her tray in her room morning and noon, and being brought to the table for dinner on my father's arm when neither Paul nor I was available or amenable to perform the chore. An artist at broadcasting her disillusionment with the food served, she manipulated her prominent nose and mouth so that no spoken word was required: "If this is the best you can do, I'll eat it, but...." Beverages were never hot enough, seasoning never sharp enough. In her "Conversations with Flossie," Edith Heal records Flossie's awareness of her mother-in-law's hostility:

> In 1927 we took the boys to Switzerland to put them in school for a year. Bill came back but I stayed. Oh boy did his mother resent it when I came back. [...] One summer Mrs. Williams was at the shore and while she was gone I had an operation. When she returned and I met her at the door her first

> words were, "Well, I never thought I'd see you again." She was always making nasty jabs about my being half German—she'd find things in the paper and send them down with Lucy, "Give *that* to Mrs. Williams."[4]

Thus, for a period of 17 years, in his own bailiwick, would be conducted a subtle but nonetheless vicious campaign of hate between the two most important female figures in his life.

4

"Dear Bo"

Meanwhile, outside the domestic triangle of Mamma, Pop, and Willie, there orbited a male satellite, Edgar Irving Williams, the younger son and brother and a horse of a completely different color. No introvert he. Tall, dark, and handsome—a superb athlete—his speaking voice a low baritone, he was a natural clothes horse who exuded maleness. This was later brought to a peak during World War I when in his leather puttees, visored military cap and fitted jacket with leather accessories he served with the American Expeditionary Forces in northern Italy.

The two boys were born within a year of each other, were classmates in Rutherford, Geneva, and Paris, and they commuted together to Horace Mann. They had always been pals, played on the same teams, Dad the pitcher and Ed the catcher, dated the same girls, and corresponded regularly when Dad was at UPenn and Ed at MIT, and also during the three years when Ed was in Rome. They took long walks together and traveled together through Italy in 1910.

Edgar, too, cared about Mamma but in a much more earthy way, as when he wrote penny postcards home from school at Boston Tech:

Oct. 16, 1905

Dear Ma:

Do I like homemade cakes and jellies? Well I guess, yes!

Ed

The card was cleverly illustrated with a drawing of Edgar burning the midnight oil.[1]

"Happy genius of my household"

Oct. 26, 1905

Dear Folks:

The box came this morning. Gee! It's great. There's no use talking, nothing can beat the home production.

Love from Edgar

Nov. 4, 1907

Dear Bo:

[...] Tell Mama to send my allowance. [...] I'm sending some football goods prepaid because I'm busted.

Ed

A regular postcard to his brother Bo:

Nov. 27, 1911

I am surely having one swell time. Paris is wonderful. Aunt Eliza sends her love. I have an awful crush on her. Gosh I'm having a fine time. Honest to John.

Ed.

Mon dieux comme c'est beau! J'aime mon vieux Paris.

Edgar was the quintessence of the All American Boy who loves Mom's cooking, is always broke, plays football, and sends home his dirty uniforms, has a crush on an older woman (who is not his mother), uses the current American slang expletives, moans about his college work schedule, but shows no lovey-dovey, mushy, sentimental emotion, thank you.

In later years, the family grapevine would have it that Ed was his mother's favorite. While living at 9 Ridge Road in the 1930s, Nana enjoyed no more effective tranquilizer than a visit from Edgar, who one or two evenings a week would drop out of the commuter parade while hoofing it up Park Avenue homeward bound to 131 West Passaic from the Rutherford railway station.

Uncle Ed was so great an athlete he made his opponents jealous. I recall sitting in the old splintery, pitch-oozing bleachers on a Sunday afternoon, early twenties, watching the Unitarians play St. Mary's.

Dad and Ed were the battery for the Unitarians, and Ed had been having a ball slapping pitches to all fields. The St. Mary's pitcher, name of Meany, became understandably peeved, and the next time Ed came to bat, he threw a high hard one at his head. Before Ed could pick himself up out of the dirt, Dad was halfway to the mound with fire in his eyes and curses on his tongue. Both benches emptied and the protagonists were squelched.

Our home always featured paintings that Ed gave Dad for Christmas. These included a diptych of the columns at Girgenti in Sicily at dawn and at dusk, a steepled church on Route 46 near Rutherford, and a graceful fountain sketched during his travels. He was a superb watercolorist, and his works did not suffer by being exhibited on the same walls with Demuth, Sheeler, Hartley, and Shahn. But Ed was a conservative, a student of classical architecture, with little patience for the radical and the *outre*.

Uncle Ed's attitude toward his brother's work had always been one of smiling understanding and tolerance—give-the-boy-plenty-of-rope-and-he'll-hang-himself sort of thing. But one morning a volume of Dad's poems that he had been at pains to deliver to Ed's home appeared in our mailbox, apparently placed there by Edgar on his daily trip to the house en route to the 7:52 to New York on the Erie.[2] There was an accompanying letter describing the book's contents as vulgar and immoral, incomprehensible balderdash, and something that he, Ed, would not tolerate in his home.[3] It was a painful experience to be rebuffed by his brother.

But the bond between the two was never broken. The year after Edgar deposited at the University of Pennsylvania the letters of his brother to him, he sent a description of his epistolary relationship with his brother dated March 19, 1966, and titled "The Story of the W.C.W. Letters to E.I.W."

> From 1902, when my brother William Carlos Williams went away to college, until 1912, when I returned from a three year period of study in Italy, we carried on a lively exchange of letters. [...] They were warm brotherly expressions of affectionate understanding as we explored the great legacy of the arts. We somehow or other depended upon one another in checking our reactions to the richness of what we found ourselves privileged to experience.
>
> Our correspondence by no means ended there. It lasted all our life until Bill died in 1963.

"Happy genius of my household"

As small boys we went to school the same day, although Bill was a year older than I. We were in the same class up to the time he went away to college. We played on the same teams, we shared the same excitement in the arts, running around the museums in Paris as kids, or hearing the first opera. This bond never left us.

Bill was the radical, I the conservative, but we had no quarrel on the importance of the arts and the humility truth carries with it. He was real and I loved him.

I kept all Bill's letters. [...] I have never given any of Bill's manuscripts except to him. If he saw fit to have given any away I have no remorse. Bill could have my shirt.[4]

5

"Put Foot"

Dad knew how to walk and enjoyed it. He could, as his father so aptly expressed it in his West Indian patois, "put foot." He grew up in a time when walking was in. He and his father and brother walked hundreds of miles for the fun of it. Penny postcards bearing Edgar's sketches of landmarks along their route to Lake George and beyond document their ability as hikers. They walked from Rutherford to West Haven, Connecticut, by circuitous routes that took them through the northwestern part of the state, stopping at inns and farmhouses along the way for meals and bed. Dad himself between 1900 and 1910 would take a trolley out of town, six, eight, or ten miles and then walk back, observing and later recording at home in his card file the various fauna and flora encountered and studied during the walk.

Now when it is customary for well-nourished and optimally muscled young athletes to drive an automobile anywhere from 1,500 meters or less to schools, playing grounds, theaters, malls, places of worship, and establishments licensed to dispense assorted varieties of grog, it may very well prove incomprehensible that there was a time when men and women less well-endowed physically would of necessity *walk* to the practice field, classes, the A&P, the library, the movies, and the girlfriend's house.[1] It would seem that man's primordial mode of transportation is in danger of becoming extinct, or at least so atrophied through disuse that we will revert to our ancient ancestral habit of locomotion on all fours. The feet, like the pineal gland and vermiform appendix (I hesitantly also suggest the brain), may very well become anatomical curiosities. These pitiful little appendages somewhere below the knee joints (on which we will be walking, the knee joints that is) will provide another lucrative piece of meat for our surgical brethren to amputate, if only for aesthetic reasons, like nose jobs; or in arctic climes, to forestall frostbite and subsequent gangrene (smells bad). Chiropodists will of necessity shift from pedicure to manicure, thereby initiating internecine war with the beauticians. Only the very poor will have functional feet because they will never be able to afford a car. And this is very fortunate, because their only medical coverage will be Medicaid, and no one would accept a patient with Medicaid!

I exaggerate for a purpose. Today the art of walking is practiced by a small minority of enthusiasts. I speak not of the pros, the heel-and-toe wobblers with piston-like arm action; the ubiquitous joggers with their labored gait and pained faces; nor the post-myocardial infarct victim cautiously doing their therapeutic mileage. I refer rather to that oddity, a man or woman who delights in walking just for the fun of it. A guy or gal who says "Let's walk up the mountain so we can enjoy the view," or "It's snowing like the devil and I love to walk in the snow." Recreational walking can be aesthetically satisfying, physically invigorating, and an escape. Granted, our urban streets and parks no longer feature elm-shaded walks nor grassy village greens. Rather, the panorama features beer cans, soda bottles, and the wrappers of fast-food joints in variety ad nauseam.Not much better the rural experience. Where once were dirt lanes and asphalt-topped "main roads" there are now four-to-eight-lane express interstate highways, and the little secondary roads are lined with fences and signs. "Beware the Dog," "Keep Out," and recently along a river in Colorado, "NO FISHING. DON'T ASK!"

In spite of these limitations and hazards, the dyed in the wool will find a way, perhaps finding transportation to the end of the line and continuing on foot. I wish them well. They are a throwback to former days. And I have no hope of converting the modern car fanatic from an addiction to auto travel to using the pedal extremities for that which the Lord intended them. The modern youth is not interested in the past. They do not look back. Its heroes are artificially created by the media. How much of a punk they have become was demonstrated in the recruits drafted for military service in the recent wars. My ridiculously hyperbolic image of foot atrophy through disuse will alert no one. The walker is hereby declared an endangered species.

But it was not always so! In the early years of this century, William George Williams, and sons William Carlos and Edgar Irving Williams, did take some walks together which are well documented by the sketches son Edgar made on the classical United States penny postal card of those years. It bore the picture of President McKinley on the stamp in one corner, and the American eagle in the opposite upper left-hand corner. In the late summer or early fall of the years 1907 and 1908, for instance, these three took off from Rutherford up the Hudson Valley and across into Massachusetts and Connecticut, interspersed here and there by rides on river ferries and "rinky-dink" railroads. The walking was purposeful, starting with Pop Williams's declaration of "put foot," the expression he carried from Santo Domingo. The three of them, with their canes would line out in a widely spaced single column! From Edgar's reports to his mother, one must conclude they marched efficiently, over 20 miles a day.

Sometimes William George Williams was away on a business trip, as in 1906 when Edgar and Bill with three friends walked to Lake George in the Adirondacks. From Fort Edward, New York, on September 3, 1906, Edgar sent a long letter to his mother because heavy rain had put a stop to their progress for that day:

> We did twenty six miles yesterday. We had the alternative of doing the whole distance or only half of it for the two towns are far apart. When we hit this place we were very tired. I was so stiff after supper I could hardly get upstairs and judging from the way the other fellows walked they were as bad as I. Bill was. We turned in at seven o' clock and I can hardly conceive of the manner in which the stiffness has left me. It's wonderful. Bill says exactly the same thing and so do the rest. Bill wants me particularly to impress upon you the fact that he feels great.
>
> Oh say! This country is fine![2]

At the end of the letter Ed quickly sketches the five walkers as "About the way we hit Fort Edward," and "we are now in Fort Edward. Twenty-six miles today."

Willie (though Ed was now calling him Bill) sent a card of Ford Edward Collegiate Institute to his mother with a brief note that said, "Rain! Rain! Rain! and only four [forty]-seven miles to Lake George. Willie." Ed sent the final, jubilant postcard of that trip on Thursday, September 6, 1906, from Moriah, New York: "We will be home Saturday morning. Things have gone perfectly. We are within three miles of our destination. Feel[s] like 100 miles more. Ed."

A well-documented trip of the trio of father and sons started on September 6, 1908, with "Sloatsburg, N.Y. First Night! Pop, Bill, Ed." Two cards, September 7, 1908: "Riverview Inn, Fishkill-on-Hudson," and "Johnsville, N.Y.—Sept. 7, 1908." This last includes a sketch of Pop and Bill stretched out in the shade. Then September 8, 1908, "Wingdale, N.Y.—40% Temp." And finally, September 9, 1908, "Botsford School House, Botsford, Conn." These cards to Raquel Williams were variously addressed with selected parts of the following:

> Mrs. W G. Williams
> Care of Mrs. Emily Wellcome
> Marine Villa, Oyster River
> Ocean Avenue
> West Haven, Connecticut

The last card from Botsford was never mailed, Edgar apparently carrying it in his pocket on the last leg of the trip. All the reports home register pleasure and friendliness and appreciation of energizing walking: "We had a fine dinner at a farmhouse"; "This is our last night's lodging place. It was simply splendid"; "The weather is still perfect. We feel great." Their goal on this outing was The Cottage at West Haven where Emily Wellcome, the mother of William George, summered with the Wellcome grandsons, and where Raquel Hélène awaited their arrival.

Four years later, in the spring of 1912, angered by a dispute with his father concerning the possibility of altering the Williams home at 131 West Passaic Avenue into a two-family residence with his office on the ground floor (which his father refused to do), Dad became so incensed that he impulsively bolted from the house and took off toward Hackensack. It was about ten in the evening when he left, following what is now Route 17 North. According to his account he walked "until about two in the morning and got almost to Oradel, ten or fifteen miles up the road. Then, having cooled off, I turned around and walked home again."[3] This is a good example of the use of walking as an escape. Dad recorded other solo walks in his card index, started on April 21, 1908, with an opening entry which reads: "It seems an advantageous way to retain impressions, fleeting ideas and exact faces for easy future reference, and as these are expected to be of some value this system has been adopted."

Solo walks are reported from Rutherford in east, north, and westerly directions to towns from ten to twenty miles away. There was in those days an efficient trolley service, and I suspect his walks were initiated on the cars, and continued afoot at the end of the line. On May 2, 1909, on a walk to Boonton, he saw "dog tooth violet, Hawthorn,

(Heath), violets, saxifrage, wild mustard, hepatica, anemone, spring beauty, myrtle, wild columbine." And on the same date, separate entry: "Cherwink, White breasted nuthatch, brown thrasher, swallows, blue birds *etc.* A flock of 8 redwings feeding and flying with a flock of pigeons. As the mixed flock passed a cherry tree the blackbirds separated out."

Observations are not merely a census of bird and vegetable life, but include records of health, behavior, sounds, and location, such as:

> May 2. Wild Azalea in magnificent profusion
>
> May 3–08 Two pairs of house wrens, strange love stunt of male, flutters obliquely down from high perch to ground near female singing all the while (opposite tennis courts)
>
> May 6. Male house wren singing in back yard. Perched several times on hollow branch placed on outhouse.
>
> May 10. Screech owl on edge of Kipp's woods. Chased me darting at my head and making two clicking sounds each time. Once it made a sound between neigh of a horse and squeak of a rat. 10 PM.

He was doubtless returning from visiting Charlotte and Flossie Herman in their house on Home Avenue, which abutted Kipp's Woods.[4]

> March 1. Flock of blue birds in the most magnificent plumage I have ever seen.
>
> Field sparrow ... near river. The longest and most musical bird song I have ever heard. It is low and very sweet and faint, but of the clearest quality imaginable and long.
>
> April 3. A most remarkable sight! Ten to twenty red cross bills with their greenish maces feeding on beechnuts at the edge of Kipp's woods. Really the most startling thing I have seen for many years. The birds were quite tame so that I approached to within ten feet of many. They literally swarmed in the low trees. One would suddenly dart down to the ground and upon finding a beechnut would at once fly up into the tree, then holding the nut in its foot it would bend over parrot fashion and eat the nut slowly.
>
> May 3. Auntie Gordon's Woods. Small lance leaved blue violet in profusion ... buttercup (prob. R. Hispidus or R. fasicularis)
>
> May 13. Sweet scented white violets in consid. Quant. in a little meadow at Cherry Hill.
>
> April 24. near Hackensack marsh marigolds in considerable quantity. Very beautiful with all other vegetation around golden clumps still dormant.

These multiple expressions of his sensibility, the implantation and honing of images and sensations, the intimacy and purity of his observations were possible only from a stable, solo platform, moving slowly through the countryside. These were the experiences of one who *walks*, and I would guess often walked alone. No noisy contraption to speed him along. Not even a companion to share experience and divert attention. These were some of the cornerstones of his *things*, as in "no ideas but in things."[5] These walks we may classify as aesthetically satisfying.[6]

During his return from study in Leipzig in 1910 to his fiancée in Rutherford, he stopped over in Spain for two weeks where he walked alone, and wrote a poem about it almost half a century later, "The High Bridge above the Tagus River at Toledo"[7]:

> A young man, alone, on the high bridge over the Tagus which
>   was too narrow to allow the sheep driven by the lean,
>   enormous dogs whose hind legs worked slowly on cogs
> to pass easily...
>   (he didn't speak the language)[8]

Walking did not end with his bachelorhood. There is historical evidence of his continued interest in putting one foot in front of the other. Vacationing in Vermont at Flossie's Uncle Einar's place often required relief from the purely pastoral environment, the day's high point being the return of the cows to the barn for evening milking, or feeding the chickens and collecting the eggs. Of course, there was the social hour (tea) on the veranda every afternoon, but communication was largely in Norwegian, in which Floss was comfortable, but in which Dad could neither send nor receive. *Alors*, one climbed the mountains! Nearby Hogback and Mt. Olga were hardly a challenge. But Haystack, which we climbed as a family, and Stratton, gave one a good workout. Stratton distinguished by residue of an old mill dam, a corduroy road leading in to Stratton Pond, and Webster Cabin, one of the shelters on the Long Trail. Daniel Webster spoke there in the early nineteenth century and a crowd of thousands from the surrounding rural countryside gathered to hear this famous orator.[9] In the 1920s, the woods in the immediate vicinity still held a few frame structures and cellar holes. I recall Dad bringing back a shirt full of apples found in an old overgrown orchard. These were extraordinary fruits, very juicy, firm, and the whitest meat we had ever seen. While visiting us kids at camp in Aroostook County, Maine, in 1923, he joined us in a hike up Mt. Chase. More romantic would be the walk through Champagne country with Bill and Sally Bird in France in 1924.[10]

William George Williams taught his two sons much else besides how to "put foot." His letters evince an intense concern and affection, while his serious interest in the theater, which he probably inherited from his mother, contributed to son William's initial desire to be a playwright. Pop Williams's design of the house at 131 Passaic may have encouraged Edgar to study architecture. His reading Shakespeare and other poets aloud to his family no doubt helped prepare Willie for his avocation of poet.

But the influence of Raquel Hélène was equally significant. Following her example, her husband and two sons played musical instruments, sang, drew, and painted portraits and landscapes. Edgar became an accomplished watercolorist, was a trustee of the Metropolitan Museum of Art and president of the National Academy of Design and the Municipal Art Society of New York. The mother's influence may have been more strongly felt if only because she was continually present while the traveling papa was elsewhere for the greater part of Dad's formative years. His mother's brother, Carlos, a Paris educated physician was the apple of Hélène's eye, and her total support after the death of her parents. He had returned from France to their home in Puerto Rico, later moving to Santo Domingo, and finally, with his sister safely married to my grandfather, migrated to the mainland, first to Panama and later to Ecuador. Young Will was impressed by Mama, with whom he always had a close spiritual relationship, to continue the "tradition" and become a physician. On the other hand, Pop, the wandering agent, having a very fuzzy familial *anlage* that his mother, Grandma Wellcome, would never divulge, certainly could bring no pressure based on family precedent. Pop was, however, a drug salesman on a grand scale, his whole professional life devoted to one concern, as wholesale supplier and importer of medicinals for Lanman and Kemp, 137 Water Street, New York City, founded AD 1808. This required travel to cities as widely separated and disparate as Geneva and Guayaquil, which was no small accomplishment and kept him away from home for months at a time. Express air travel to Europe and South America between 1880 and 1918, when he died, was not an option. What type of agent he was, and how familiar with medical terminology he was, I don't know, but as an indicator of some of the literature he was familiar with, I quote a letter he wrote to my Dad, April 27, 1906:

> I mailed you yesterday what I think you will find a good book, consisting of extracts from Dr. Osler's writings. [...] I read an article lately, from the London Lancet I think, in which it said that it is a fallacy to suppose that an unlimited amount of mental work can be done if an equal excess of physical exercise is performed.

So we have an English gentleman papa—he never became an American citizen because his British passport was more convenient for travel in South America—conversant to some extent with medical literature, apparently for business purposes. Somehow I doubt this was ever a factor in my father's decision to become a physician. On the other hand, I feel Mama leaned heavily on her son Will to emulate his Uncle Carlos. She got her wish and thereby initiated a dichotomy in his life which persisted until in late years a series of cerebral and neoplastic illnesses made it impossible for him to continue as a physician.

6

Medical Education in Leipzig, 1909–1910

The year 1909 was very critical in the life of William Carlos Williams. On March 4, William Howard Taft was inaugurated as our twenty-seventh President. At about the same time Dad found himself out on his ass at 61st Street and 10th Avenue, in New York City. The Nursery and Child's Hospital had canned him for insubordination because of his refusal to sign, as senior resident physician, a graft-loaded report to Albany.[1] Thus he became a member of the unemployed. "I had no idea where I was headed," he recalls in his autobiography. "[A]n altogether idyllic moment."[2]

He wrote, directed, and presented a play "on the embankment at the Rutherford Town Tennis Club," and quite serendipitously "first observed Flossie, the kid, on Park Avenue [the main drag] in Rutherford, and my whole life came to a head."[3] He had his first book of poems published by a local printer, Reid Howell, at his own expense.[4] He apparently neglected his correspondence with brother Edgar who, on May 7, sent a card of complaint. He wandered by the Passaic River and did some painting.

Concurrently there were daily trysts with Florence Hilda Herman, "the kid," who would conditionally accept his proposal of marriage as he took ship for Germany a few months later. Brother Edgar, in Boston studying architecture, had won the Prix de Rome, a scholarship for three years to study in the Italian capital. Pop Williams had promised young Will he would pay his way for a year of postgraduate medical study abroad if Ed won, and "Ed co-operated, as usual."[5]

I suspect Pop Williams, viewing the influences tearing at the flesh of his firstborn, was quite delighted to see him shake off the dust of Rutherford—play directing, poetry publishing, girl courting, nature walking—and get back, though still seething about his hospital dismissal, on the track of his medical career. And I would assume our hero himself had no trouble acquiescing with the decision.

His choice was a year in Germany, which was rapidly succeeding France and England as the foremost center of medical progress. It was there, for instance, that Paul Ehrlich announced his discovery of Salvarsan 606, the famous arsenical for treatment of syphilis. Our hero himself later said, however, he chose Leipzig because he "had been in love with the concert pianist who had spent three years there at the Conservatory."[6] The pianist was Charlotte, "the kid's" much older sister, and Edgar's fiancée for two years while he was in Italy, the disengagement occurring by mutual consent. And so he crossed the Atlantic on a second-class ship, making landfall at Gravesend, England, on August 4, 1909, whence he sent a card to "the kid," and followed with others.

> Dear Floss,
>
> Great trip! Not sea sick a bit. Lots of fun on the way. You cannot imagine the thrill I felt on seeing England the home of my shopkeeper or noble ancestors as the case may be. I'm sun burnt; my hair stands up as the bristles of a broom. I haven't worn a cap for days. On Thursday, Aug 5, I arrive Antwerp. I did not fall seriously in love many times on the trip.
>
> Billie

August 10, 1909, to Florence Herman:

> I always think of you when I see the Thomas Kirsche because you spoke of it in your last letter to me. Gee but I'm lonely that's all I can say but if I ever etc. ad lib.

This is followed by a second card same date:

> What I was going to say is that if I ever meet a foreigner in my country after this he can have anything I've got. Best, best wishes.
>
> Billie

On August 14 he sent a tinted postcard, titled "Leipzig, Marchenbrunnem" ("Fairytale Fountain"), which shows a grotto with a youth proffering a hat full of water to his girl companion:

> Lord how glad I am that I can't get old! For to feel that I could lose the joy of my little counter part in this picture would be misery to me. I fairly worship this group. Billie

6. Medical Education in Leipzig, 1909–1910

Meanwhile, back home the World Series of 1909, from October 11 to 16 was on, the first ever to go to seven games (and the year before the big league baseball contained a cork center). The Pittsburgh Pirates took the Detroit Tigers four to three, winning the last game with a six-hit shutout. I'm sure Dad's mind was on all that—he and Ed played baseball and were fans—and he'd have given a lot to see Honus Wagner at short for Pittsburgh slap the ball on Ty Cobb's face as he slid, spikes flying, into second, splitting his lip.

Then on October 19 he was in Dresden, writing to Florence: "It's great. Saw the Sistine Madonna and almost passed away it was so wonderfully pure and peaceful." Five days later he was in Leipzig again, after a Saturday night out with the boys:

> Dear Florence: Great old place this, but oh such a headache! And Sunday at that. Well I'm not cut out for the German student type and that's plain [...]. [I]f I could only kill that awful homesickness or nostalgia but it won't kill. Ta-ta. Billie.
>
> Work begins next week.

He had already been working on improving his German. He learned enough in two months to be ready for lectures and clinics in the not-quite-five-month term beginning in late October. Although already a doctor, with his MD from the University of Pennsylvania and his internship at two hospitals in New York City, he looked so youthful, all 66 kg (145 pounds), that a clerk at the Allgemeine Credit Anstalt insisted he was "*nicht Doktor, aber Student von Medizin.*"[7]

So began his postgraduate medical education. Although he had decided, while at Nursery and Childs, that pediatrics would be his specialty, his notes reveal (in a mixture of English and German) exposure to a variety of medical topics, ranging from endocrinology, cardiology and neurology to gastroenterology, and infectious diseases.

Looking at the notes I was amazed. My medical education began just 27 years later, and I can see he was living inside medical history. The physicians who were his teachers were the product of half a century of great scientific advances. They were skilled diagnosticians and pathologists. They had benefited from the work of medical pioneers such as René Laennec in physical diagnosis, Rudolf Virchow in pathology, John Hunter in physiology, Louis Pasteur and Robert Koch in bacteriology, and Joseph Lister in surgery. The German university hospitals had become the mecca for American doctors seeking panache for their professional "portfolios" before returning to the U.S. But in the light of present-day knowledge it is almost pitiful to realize the gaps in the fields of physiology and therapeutics. The word "vitamin" was not in their vocabulary, for instance, with the result that a lecture or clinic on the subject of rickets by a Professor Otto Soltmann began (to quote from the card file), "[n]o chapter in the consideration of rickets is free from strife and disagreement. [Is the cause] calcium resorption or failure of deposition? Calcium deficiency is merely an end effect." As to prognosis, the professor bluntly stated: "Do not commit the folly of saying the child will grow out of it. He will never grow out of it." As for symptomatology: "Frequence of fracture [decalcified bones], Tete Carre [square shape of the head due to bossae, 'bumps,' like the head of Frankenstein's monster], Spasmophilie [seizures, or convulsions due to calcium deficiency]." And as for medicine's future in combatting the disease, "when we know the 'biochemie' of the deposition of calcium in bones, we will know more about rickets—not until then." Naturally there was no mention of Vitamin D, which was to be the cure but was not isolated by Elmer Verner McCollum until 1925. Yet the antirachitic effect of fish oil (I can taste it yet) was indeed appreciated, not only in Germany but in the medical world generally.

There was also recognition of other deficiency states, which would later be associated with the lack of certain foods, and would be compensated for by rice polishings for beriberi, citric juices for scurvy, etc. Not until 1936 was Vitamin B1—thiamine—synthesized; not until 1928 was Vitamin C constructed in the laboratory. Dad's instructors in Leipzig, 1909, were well aware of the gaps in their knowledge, and at this distance their capacity to assemble the jigsaw puzzle of these diseases, without the missing final piece, seems remarkable.

And Dad fully appreciated their skill and dedication, especially that of Soltmann. In his notes for December 11, he makes this observation: "Soltmann's 65th birthday. His beautiful character. Love for teaching, and for children, and for humor." My curiosity aroused, I undertook to find out something about Soltmann's career through Professor Joachim Sartorius of Berlin, who is currently translating and publishing the works of William Carlos Williams into German.[8] He in turn put me in touch with Christopher Sorger, a scholar, whose thoroughgoing research followed Soltmann from his birth in Berlin in 1844 to his death in 1912 (Michael Gozdeski translated the German for me).

Soltmann's medical studies had taken him from Berlin to Wurzburg, Prague, and Vienna. In Vienna he developed his interest in pediatrics. He initially practiced in Breslau, finally settling in Leipzig. Here, as professor of pediatrics, he became involved in state and local politics, and it is unclear whether he was ever granted tenure. The City Council of Leipzig wrote the Ministry of Culture of the Kingdom of Saxony (1907) that he should have it—he was then 63—since he headed both the Leipzig Children's Clinic and the Polyclinic. He had given these institutions service without pay for years, and the tenured appointment would at least provide him and his chief of surgery with a salary of sorts. So admired were his services that the *Oberburgermeister* ("Mayor") felt that the clinic, under Soltmann, should be the prototype for Germany. *The Yearbook for Pediatrics* following his death, besides mentioning the thousands of children he had treated, noted that he had conducted research on the nervous systems of newborns, had written a textbook on nervous disorders of children, and published articles on diet and special treatments for children. He also wrote about problems of hospitals and statistics. *The Yearbook* also noted that he was a "*liebensvurdigen, frohlich Gesellschafter*" ("an amiable, happy associate").

Further in Dad's notes, Soltmann, in lecturing on infectious diseases of childhood, begins: "Scarlet fever most to be feared of all diseases of childhood. Nephritis can be and is avoided by remaining in bed for several weeks." In this he again shows his clinical acumen but also his lack of ultimate knowledge of the systemic involvement by the strep toxin. And further on, differentiating between various diseases, he opens with these curious observations:

> Beginning of scarlet resembles diphtheria.
> Beginning of measles resembles pertussis.

These connections were unfamiliar to me from my student days in the 1930s, but they certainly make sense. Both scarlet fever and diphtheria display a primary lesion in the throat, and each produces a painful pharyngitis, with exudate and membranous lesions on the tonsils. Each may also produce extremely ill patients, with high fever and marked "toxicity." The throat culture, yielding corynebacterium diphtherium for diphtheria and group A beta hemolytic strep for scarlet, are the definitive diagnostic tests.[9] These procedures were available to the clinicians of 1909, as was diphtheria antitoxin for the former, but the availability of penicillin, so important for the treatment of both diseases, would have to await the discovery, by a curious British bacteriologist, of a fungus growing on his culture plate that inhibited the growth of streptococci.[10]

Similarly insightful was the simile between pertussis (whooping cough to the uninitiated) and measles because at onset each has a characteristic severe cough. To the current crop of medical graduates this will have little significance, since in our time almost all children are immunized, and the paroxysms of pertussis have become an endangered species. No longer the wards of whoopers like those Philip Stimson showed us at the old Willard Park Hospital on Avenue D at the foot of Manhattan. Dr. Stimson maintained that the cough of pertussis was infectious, in the sense that one coughing child would start the whole ward into paroxysms. I can recall hanging at the ward entrance disbelieving, when sure enough one kid coughed and like a train of dominos around the ward it went, a dozen or more kids whooping, strangling, and puking. The cough of measles is also severe, due perhaps to the enanthem, or bronchial inflammation; and often, as Soltmann suggested, it is the symptom that ushers in the disease.

But in a matter of hours other findings make the differential apparent, pertussis having an indolent, drawn-out course, while measles on the other hand demonstrates cough, coryza, conjunctivitis, koplik spots, and rash in rapid-fire order. In 1909, as in 1950, the feared complication was pneumonia and, at the turn of the century, invasion of the lung fields with tuberculosis. This was true for both pertussis and measles.

Tuberculosis or TB was then endemic throughout the civilized world, and the kiss of death for indigenous peoples when the white man intruded. In 1909, in suburban Rutherford spitting on the sidewalk was a misdemeanor punishable by a fine because TB was a disease transmitted by aerosolized sputum from a consumptive. In 1909, in Leipzig, it was taught that the pediatric TB patient was particularly at risk when confined within the four walls of a home with other residents. The latter were encouraged to escape to fresh air and sunlight, leaving the unfortunate infant closeted with their "problem." Debate was continuing as to the primary site of infection, whether pulmonary or intestinal, as well as the type of bacillus, whether bovine or human. The topic of the clinic on January 9, 1910, was "*Porschingen uber die Aetiologie der Tuberclose,*" with differing explanations of two authorities, Emil von Behring and

Robert Koch, being discussed concerning the disease's onset. The bacillus of TB had been definitely determined by Koch, but portal of entry and type of bacillus, human or bovine, was still being debated. Behring maintained that pulmonary TB was a "*schluss* phase from an abdominal infection in childhood from cows' milk. Koch says cows' milk is not dangerous." Initially Koch's views were *widersprachen* ("opposed, contradicted") "but after many experiments they are not overthrown but so *beschrankt* ['limited'] as not to have pract. imp." This statement was further investigated; "a commission found that, in sixty-eight cases dead of TB, only eight showed the bovine type of bacillus, then concluded it was not dangerous!" Dad's exclamation point. And then there was the climactic case at end of rounds: "[...] two days unconscious. Basilar TB meningitis. Eyes up. teeth clenched, head back"—the classic opisthonic posture of terminal meningitis.

An authoritative contribution to the subject of TB was kindly provided at my request by Dr. Jeffrey Boscamp, who examined Dad's notes, was much impressed, and reacted at length. Dr. Boscamp's specialty is infectious diseases, and among his observations were these:

> An elementary classification of mycobacteria was already taking place in these notes, years before [Ernest] Runyan would classify them based on growth characteristics: "bird variety grows much quicker than human!" Interestingly they (the Leipzig teachers) were not far off when considering the differences between TB from cows, birds and humans. There has been no doubt for some time now that these are distinct species of mycobacteria, but for years the "bird type," now called mycobacteria avium-intracellulare, was an obscure organism of little clinical significance [...].
>
> Little did [your father] know on Jan 29, 1910, that his "bird variety" would reappear as a clinically significant and devastating pathogen in the AIDS epidemic of the 1980s.

Jeff Boscamp's detailed observations, together with another kindly "consultant" I applied to, Dr. Damon Fellman, confirmed my impression that the contents of the Leipzig lectures and clinics were much the same as I was taught at Cornell Medical College 27 years later. After studying Dad's notes I could no longer feel, as I had before, that his medical education dated back to the dark ages. But not trusting my own judgment I consulted my younger colleagues. Medical education, 40 years after my own and at the end of the twentieth century, was needed to confirm the worth of what Dad learned in Leipzig. In general, my consultants helped me to see that it was not so much the "science" of medicine but the "art" of medicine in Dad's notes that impressed us all. Dr. Boscamp specifically noted that "the descriptions of disease [in Dad's notes] are now classic" and show that

> indeed, physicians were measured by this [descriptive] ability. [Thus] the notes of Feb 11, 1910, praise a physician as "one of the most competent and exact observers of our time." The powers of observation and description were traits which modern physicians have lost in this era of technological diagnosis.

Dr. Fellman, a neurologist, "was most impressed with the skillful drawings and the appearance of unhurried attention to detail and concept. Neatly organized. Attractive jotting that bears no resemblance to any medical school notes that I have seen or written." However, there were great unknowns: "Surgery is of doubtful value" (December 4, 1909). And "Of course there is absol. nothing known" (December 6, 1909).

> At the turn of the century no blood tests, electrocardiograms or antibiotics [were available, and there was] limited availability of primitive x-ray. From the neurologist's point of view I note the absence of CAT scans, electroencephalograms, MRI scans, spinal tap, electrical study of nerve and muscle, evoked potentials, medication for epilepsy, meningitis or Parkinson's Disease.

When I asked Dr. Fellman whether "the early manifestations of greatness" could be found in Dad's notes, he pointed to their care with detail, and observed that he was particularly impressed with the note for December 10, 1909, on the subject of impotence:

> Formerly it was thought to be always the woman's fault but men are the cause (more often) than thought earlier. Psychic impotence [...] esp. in men who have led the life and then when they marry a pure girl are incapable. Neurasthenia (treatment); leave the genitalia alone. Treat everything except the genitalia. Make it clear that he is suffering from a nerve not a genital disease and assure him of success. (Case—sent the wife away and forbade him to go to her. Naturally he went the next day.)

Dr. Fellman then summed up his reaction:

> The point to be demonstrated is that Dr. Williams was instructed to take the role of decision-maker for his patients, including assuming a higher authority than the individual on a matter of their welfare without their express consent [...].
>
> Treatment was apparently determined by passing on the methods that

> had been successful for prior practitioners. No mention is made of controlled studies, double blind or single blind, or a logical approach to assessing the effectiveness of a treatment modality [...]. Medicare, HMOs, IPA's and other organized groups are already talking about denying payment for treatments that are not proven effective and prudent. In 1990 that means the type of controlled study that was not mentioned in your father's notes. How far we have come, probably mostly for the good, but some things are lost as well.

Both my hired guns, Drs. Boscamp and Fellman, recognized in their reading of Dad's notes a quality too little appreciated and practiced by today's physicians. As Jeff Boscamp put it, "[w]e can learn much from the physicians of that time. In the absence of curing, there can be caring. As taught in Leipzig in 1910, one can at least communicate with the patient, and 'remember to give a bad prognosis' with compassion." I think it significant that my father paid such close attention to his instructors, and that his own observational and descriptive and graphic abilities were so outstanding.

Twelve years later, having experienced private practice in the U.S., Dad was to return to Europe, specifically to the clinics of Vienna, with other "pilgrims" of many nationalities. And at that time he was to express disillusionment with American medicine. In his 1928 autobiographical novel, *A Voyage to Pagany*, the character representing Williams, named Dr. "Dev" Evans, asks himself, "[w]hat is American medicine?" And he replies: "A hodge-podge of procedure, kindly enough but no head nor tail to it, no wish to seek clarity in that mass—."[11] Then he asks what he had come to Vienna for anyway. Answer: "To perfect." Then, commenting on the other Americans attending this teaching session, and on organized medicine in general, he concludes they were mostly after "cash for cures":

> He remembered the agitant pathologist secretary of his own County Medical Society remarking—"What, not a member! Why, Evans, don't you know that no matter how fine a physician you may be, you have no standing whatever in your profession unless you are a member of your county and state societies?"—He felt nauseated at the thought. He remembered his name in little print instead of heavy print in The Directory of the American Medical Association. And he had seen the lack—the pretense and the lack—which always gave him the feeling of hopelessness that he felt before any successful cult, the horrible emptiness—the impossibility of instilling sense into piecemeal minds—gut minds—without thoughts of the limits of knowledge.[12]

Dev praises a revered instructor in Vienna, Dr. Knobloch, who had also suffered disillusionment with American medicine:

> [...] Dev began to get that sense of beauty in arrangement, that fervor which the continental scientific method, built upon their aristocratic thought, had engendered, to go far through the world. [...]
>
> Knobloch here was great. Surely it was a great love that shone in his countenance. One could understand how he had wanted to leave Vienna at the offer in cash from the University of Michigan or whichever it was, and how being in the United States a few months he could not stand it but had to flee back to Vienna—and the children's hospital where he lived.[13]

Although Dad's plaints of loneliness, celibacy, and frigid weather were tempered by his descriptions of sightseeing, visits to museums, evenings at the theater and opera, concerts at the Thomaskirche, and weekend parties, all of which seemed to gainsay that life in Leipzig was all gloom and frustration, he nevertheless left the city the day courses ended on March 2.

The two "wild" weekends he and Bill Kelly enjoyed he described in detail to his brother, and in lesser detail to Florence. On December 30, 1909, he told Ed about spending Christmas weekend in Berlin with Misses Metcalf and Smith, two American girls studying singing in Berlin. Ed had met them on the boat over and told them about his brother.

> It was one wild and continuous tear, a sort of sand storm of incidents in a German desert of dried mummies with four deleterious Arabs flitting around in the glare of gas, electricity and dabbling deliciously in beer, chocolates, oysters, raggy music, and what not for "entrée oeuvres." I never experienced such a foolishness in one red gob but oh did we not have one real good time. Why one day, it was Sunday p.m. we stood up, yes on our feet in a gradually darkening room and argued steadily for about two hours on philosophy. We started on the nature of nothing and talked till our sentences became blue flames dancing around us with nothing else visible. Such a business! It was church, cafes, concert and home one after the other indiscriminately and the girls sang well between times. We ended up sitting all huddled together on a divan with Miss Metcalf's left arm resting on my right knee while I played with her new coral bracelet and Bill Kelly was trying his best to get an opening to Miss Smith's waist with his left. All the while it was one old or new American song after another until one o'clock and then good bye.[14]

The other instance of Bacchanalian revelry occurred less than two weeks later when the two ladies came to Leipzig. Bill reported to Ed on January 9, 1910:

> She [Miss Metcalf] and Miss Smith have been visiting Leipzig you know. They were on their way to Dresden and since Friday night until today Sunday the four of us have been on another hilarious tear. It is fun, but Ach du liebe I am poorer than even a Unitarian Church Mouse. Nevertheless we had a fine time for somehow or other I'm getting on to the knack of letting money slide easy when it must, I guess it's Bill [Kelly]'s influence.[15]

Goodbye Leipzig, loneliness, German militarism, medical clinics. Hello England, France, Italy, warmer weather, friend Ezra Pound, brother Edgar. A short visit *en famille* with the Peabody family in Olney, Bucks, before returning to London for a week of Pound, including a reading by William Butler Yeats. Then on to Paris, passing a few days with Eliza Anduze, a relative of his father who apparently ranked as some sort of an aunt.[16] Meeting with disfavor in her apartment because of his reading Heinrich Heine's *Buch der Lieder* quietly to himself while lying in bed (she being strongly pro–French and anti–Kaiser Wilhelm), and finding a visit to the Comédie Française a chilling experience, he was glad to leave for sunny Italy and never forgot the thrill of "coming out of the wintry tunnel under the Alps at Domodossola and seeing the waterfalls leaping from the rocks on all sides above me in a full glory of the Italian sun. I'll never forget that! I must have been a very impressionable young man. [...] It was a bewilderment, it was incredible."[17]

Two weeks of Italy in the spring, brother Edgar acting as guide, introducing him to medieval, Renaissance, and Greek architecture and art. Siena, Paestum, Amalfi, Capri, Pompeii, and Naples, "where small boys in the street threw stones at us where we stood on the cathedral steps because we insisted on carrying our own luggage."[18] At last he was shipping out for home from Naples on an old steamer, when he had to jump ship at Gibraltar because of a self-diagnosed attack of appendicitis, and his decision to throw in his lot with the British surgeons ashore rather than gamble on the ship's doctor, whose appearance had impressed him unfavorably. His symptoms having subsided on waking at the hotel in Gibraltar the following morning, and the ship having gone on, he had perforce two weeks to kill before the next ship came around. With 60 dollars in his pocket he embarked on a two-week tour of Spain, which he describes vividly in the *Autobiography*, particularly his encounters with the "little guys," shepherds, beggars, altar boys, dancers, bar hangers.[19] These people ring so true, and certainly foretell the meat of his productions in poetry in the years to come.

That unexpected two-week sojourn over, he was back aboard ship, homeward bound to Hoboken and Rutherford, Flossie the kid, and the beginning of his medical practice in his parents' home, where he would first display a large sheet of parchment, appropriately signed and stamped with the seal of the university attesting to the presence and participation of the "Americamus ex vico Rutherford" by

Almae Universitatis
Lipsiensis
Karolo Binding, Rector

This now resides in the Rutherford Public Library.

In 1910, the year Dad returned from Leipzig, newspapers announced Paul Ehrlich's discovery of Salvarsan or 606, an arsenical treatment of syphilis. Ezra Pound—whom Dad had met at the University of Pennsylvania, and who had gone to London to write, and save, poetry—was visiting my father in Rutherford in late 1910, having returned from Philadelphia because of a case of jaundice. Pound suggested that the two of them buy a carload of 606 when it became available and hie themselves off to North Africa. "Between us, I with my medical certificate and experience, he with his social proclivities, we might, he thought, clean up a million treating all the wealthy old nabobs there—presumably rotten with the disease—and retire to our literary enjoyments within, at most, a year."[20] Pop Williams torpedoed this scheme. Ehrlich was one of Dad's medical heroes. A graduate of Leipzig, in 1878, he had written his thesis on dyes and stains in medicine, had continued his research on that subject, and won a Nobel Prize in Medicine in 1908. For his discovery of Salvarsan he was nominated for a second Nobel in 1915 but died before it could be awarded.

Because Edgar's Prix de Rome lasted three years, the letters to and from Bill permit us a glimpse of his courtship of Flossie. Not only were the letters to Edgar frequent, but Bill promised that the wedding would not occur until Ed was home again. Bill to Edgar, June 10, 1910:

> Since I have been here I have seen Charlotte and Florence. There is no mistake about their caliber they are as different from the rag tag of this country as Rome is from Hoboken. I gave Charlotte your kiss and the little necklace and Florence has the little ribbon.
>
> Florence has not let me kiss her and in short and few she does not intend to let me do so for "many years" as she put it which is wise but inconvenient.

She tells me I am "perfectly free" to come and go as I please, she will give me no answer and there the game stands.[21]

Flossie was 20 years old on April 18, 1910, more than seven years younger than her fiancé. It is obvious from the letters that they were fascinated with each other and intended that their love would last their entire lives. Bill to Edgar on July 5, 1910:

As to that kid Florence, there is a great deal and yet nothing to say. I see her about three or four times a week and I see her alone about once a week. Ah Bo it's the best feeling a man can ever have to know that this similar but yet totally different little human creature beside him is just tingling with total sympathy for his very thoughts before he can think them. Love is the solid foundation on which the rest builds. It is a great inspiration to feel and believe that nothing can take this love from you, that no matter what may happen that at least is always ready to bear and to support. [...]

[...] It is this that is new to me for in the past tho' I have cared for several girls I could not imagine them as growing old and feeble and sick perhaps and still being as dear to me as ever. Any slip they made in manners or other ways offended me horribly and I immediately felt a falling away of my affection for them but now I feel as tho' it were a fault of my own when this little girl makes foolish breaks and unconsciously offends against certain forms in one way or another. I feel as if it were myself who is at fault and at once I plan how we together shall improve ourselves. This is a wonderful experience.[22]

7

The Physical

He was about five feet nine inches tall, shoe size 8D, hat size 7¼, shirt size 15½-32, waist 32 to 34, with good posture in both standing and sitting positions.[1] His weight fluctuated between 145 and 165 pounds and was well distributed. The shoulder girdles were well developed and the pectorals completely concealed the rib cage. His abdomen was flat, his legs just missed being skinny.

His arms were generously muscled, and I recall as a tad his ability to throw a walking stick high up into a hickory or chestnut tree to bring down a shower of nuts for us kids. His hands were spade-like, "a ditch-digger's hands," he used to say, with blunt-tipped fingers and calloused palms. He was always clean-shaven. I can't seem to recall more than a single day's beard on his face, until in his late years his illnesses crippled him, and he made do with an electric shaver.

The unruly jet-black hair epitomized in his self-portrait gradually gave way to baldness and an encircling halo of gray at the periphery of his skull. His eyes were dark brown, always searching, looking not only at you, but into you; nor impolitely, but in an interested kind of way. I know it made my eldest daughter, Emily, uncomfortable to be under his gaze when she was a toddler. There was nothing distinguished about his mouth, just a horizontal opening in his face paralleling the lower edge and completing the square of his moderately protruding chin.

His dominating facial feature of course was his nose, which he recognized and early on glorified in his 1917 poem "Smell!" addressed to "Oh strong-ridged and deeply hollowed / nose of mine!"[2] It was his most characteristic facial feature, with a dromedary hump halfway down. A snapshot taken by his brother Ed in the arena at Fiesole around 1910 shows a classic John Barrymore profile, the office girl's romantic hero. These physiognomic features were spaced appropriately on a skin of

William Carlos Williams in the Roman amphitheater at Fiesole outside Florence, 1910. Courtesy the Poetry Collection of the University Libraries, University at Buffalo, The State University of New York.

slightly olive hue, weathered in later years and peppered liberally, particularly on the brow and temples, with pigmented nevi.

He walked with his toes slightly inverted, a custom encouraged in those days. To walk Indian style was to walk well. His gait was purposeful. You felt he had a goal in mind as he strode along. This you can feel in the photo, well published.[3] Dad in his old Panama, leaving the "old" Rutherford library, probably returning from the post office, which he habitually visited a half dozen times a day, getting off copy to publishers and letters to aspiring writers seeking advice.

He needed physical work for an outlet. The sweating body smeared with dirt gave respite to that seething brain. There was about him an aura of tension, an invisible halo of potential that demanded a constant release. His sleep requirement was minimal, and he apparently derived as much refreshment from a quick 40 winks on the living room couch as you and I might have from half a night's sleep.

So how to sum up? How to put a caul over this many-tentacled animal and put him on display? He was an average physical sample of homo sapiens living in an average suburban community who was distinguished from his neighbors because he happened to be a physician.

The fact that he was an artist created not even a ripple on the surface of the pond that was Rutherford in the first half of the twentieth century. Furthermore, few other than some close intimates realized that boundless energy he possessed and how generous he was in spending it on his patients, his art, and his fellow artists, and those who aspired to become fellow artists. A human guy who had something for everyone. "Human" by definition is imperfection. What he had for some was positive and perfect, even irresistible. For others it might be neutral or imperfect. But he wasn't a neutron. His vibes touched everyone who came in contact with him. He was approachable, attracting many different kinds of people for many different reasons. His was a magnetic physical presence.

8

Food

Dad enjoyed eating. For him it was a pleasurable necessity.[1] He was neither gourmet nor gourmand, but ate with relish and gusto what was served him. Soup was blown and "supped." The soft-boiled egg in the morning was eaten from the shell in an egg cup, and the last trace of white was scraped down to the amniotic membrane before it was put aside. The ingestion of celery was a jam session, with the masseter and temporal muscles at the sides of the face, rhythmically rising and falling, setting the tempo. A rib bone was to be chewed clean. A seafood dinner of steamers and lobster was a full symphony. Each clam stripped, washed in the broth, dunked in butter, and engorged, to be followed by the bits of white muscle painstakingly scraped from each shell, and the last shred chased by the cup of broth, which was drained to the sandy dregs. The lobster was crushed, dismembered, stripped, picked, and sucked down to the most distal segment of the hindmost appendage. Only a cup of shards remained to be returned to the kitchen. Each leaf of an artichoke was repeatedly flensed, leaving only shreds of the cellulose supporting structure to be discarded. At the end the cleansed heart of the plant, submerged in the residual of the melted butter, was impaled and mouthed with a final flourish. His attack on an apple was an explosion. His strong functional teeth were buried like a mechanical clam shell in the meat of the fruit, and as the juices jetted laterally like the squirt of a disturbed piss clam, a wedge was ripped out, including a portion to the core, and the whole joyously masticated as he wiped the cidery froth from his chin on the back of his forearm. He was a vigorous and happy trencherman, and yet not lacking in decorum. Quite regularly he bit the inside of his cheek at the peak of the feast.

Mom was a good cook. Her kitchen was efficiently administered, and the food was respected and tastefully prepared. At all meals the table was nicely set. Serving dishes came from the kitchen piping hot, their savory steam providing us a preview of their contents. The job was well done, and I think Mom knew it. No need for hyperbole on Dad's part. Yet I feel the onus of the daily prospect of three square meals for an adult male and two growing sons was lightened for her by his wordless gustatory approbation. Was this perhaps a subtle form of lovemaking?

Smell and taste, those symbiotic senses triggered by the receptors embedded in the lining of nose and mouth were actively working partners. His was a big nose, capable of sampling a more than generous aliquot of his environment. He pointedly smelled everything. A new book, a mushroom, a cow, a urine sample, the air about him, and his own armpit were sampled olfactorily and thus given an added dimension. Isolated in a strange place, I think his first action in orienting himself would be to smell it. Charles Lamb would have understood.[2] And smell's Siamese twin, taste, never was permitted to lose its tone. There were moments when we stood aghast at his temerity in tasting. A simple walk in the countryside became a laboratory session for the taste buds. We tasted the buds and twigs of the wild cherry, sassafras, birch, and witch hazel. We dug and pulled to obtain the thumb-sized morsel in the heart of the common pasture fern that dots New England's pastures. The white, crisp, nutty slip of embryonic tissue was adequate reward for the time and energy expended. We sampled the sap of the maple in spring and found it wanting. We hacked off and chewed the gum of the spruce. Besides the traditionally edible wild berries, we sampled the barberry, wintergreen berries, bunch berries, shad or service berries, rose hips, and the beautiful red fruit with the black umbilicus that adorns the yew in the fall. Granted almost everything we tried was known to be the natural food of some bird or beast. But there were times when Dad alone did the sampling.

At Hilldale, Mom's Uncle Einar's farm outside of Wilmington in Vermont, we gathered milk pails full of mushrooms. These were taken back to the house and studied with the help of a book on the subject. We knew most of the poisonous ones on sight, but while in the field we'd occasionally come upon a stranger, and Dad would peel the top and take a nip from the edge of the spore-nearing cap. This would be diced daintily between the incisors and ingested. Just a sample, you understand, the theory being that it wasn't an Amanita, and the other poisonous varieties were for the most part only emetic and would merely induce vomiting. He stubbornly maintained that he was one of those for whom the emetic Russula was non-poisonous. Yet on at least one occasion when Mom, with considerable reservations, cooked him an assorted batch of his gatherings of mushrooms, he was shortly thereafter compelled to vomit.

But acute indigestion, at least after his marriage, was not a chronic problem. In general, he had an ironclad gut that mangled, absorbed, and excreted everything that came its way in uncomplaining routine. In his bachelor days, on the other hand, he had been subject to frequent digestive disorders, and Mom attributes them to the diet in his parents' home. His mother was certainly an adequate cook, but her culinary background was strictly West Indian, and her dietary staples were beans and rice. His English father demanded his ration of beef, but cooked beyond recognition with the last trace of blood purged, leaving a colorless, flavorless, and, at least for Dad, indigestible residue. His description of the table spread for the house staff during his internship in New York is certainly no prescription for a griping belly. Whether organic or psychosomatic, his complaints were cured by marriage and Mom's home cooking. In the years I lived with him and shared his table, the only digestive aids I knew him to take was an occasional slug of rhubarb and soda for overindulgence, and a rare ounce of castor oil for the usual indication.

Butter as an adjunct to any meal was a recognized staple in our diet in Dad's time—to him the meal was planned around the butter dish. A dash in the eggshell along with the salt to lace the flavor. A copious smear on all bread products to lubricate the track. An ear of corn swam in the stuff. A mound of mashed potatoes was cratered with a yellow oleaginous lake. Baked potato skins became butter sandwiches. Butter was the last item removed from our table, because the desert, no matter its character, just might be improved by a touch of butter. "Just leave the butter please, Lucy." His addiction was a standing family joke. I suppose Dad suffered during the days of rationing in 1917 until his fairy godmother took a hand. While driving one day on an outlying street he came upon a packing case in the middle of the road. Considering it a traffic hazard, he stopped, lifted it into the back of the car, and continued on his way. Exploration later at home revealed enough oleomargarine to feed a battalion for a week. Judicious doctoring with salt and food coloring yielded a product sufficiently like butter so that we were able to prevent Dad's having withdrawal symptoms until the real stuff was obtainable again.

"Happy genius of my household"

I suppose it's axiomatic that where there is good food there is good booze. There was always liquor available at 9 Ridge Road, but except for parties at New Year's Eve or other festive occasions, it was used most temperately. Cocktails in the evening before dinner (martinis, except for occasional frozen daiquiris in very hot weather) were the standard fare. Dad's limit was usually one. Wine at meals was for guests and special occasions. During Prohibition there was good grain alcohol available on prescription, and Flossie transmuted it into good gin with juniper drops and charcoal filters. Patients from the Italian colony in Lyndhurst would settle an old account by bringing crates of grapes and crushing them in a huge hogshead in the basement. Eventually there evolved gallons of purple wine in bottles of assorted sizes and ancestry. At Flossie's mother's place at Monroe there was Nannie's special home brew that would hit the ceiling in the dining room when uncapped at the table. In France the folks enjoyed a walking tour of Burgundy and Champagne with Bill and Sally Bird, sampling as they went.

Roy, the bootlegger, was a regular caller at Ridge Road, bringing everything from scotch to applejack. He later ran a clam bar in Nutley on the riverbank and would show up every New Year's Day about noon with a sack of oysters over his shoulder. After a slug of beef tartare and some black coffee he'd open as many oysters as Mom wanted (usually several dozen) and then take off for the next friend's house. No charge. I suppose it was he who brought into the house a pint flask of whiskey labeled "Panther Piss," the label displaying a lascivious-looking panther with lolling tongue and a tremendous reproductive organ dangling below and dripping golden drops of "piss." This sounds as if the property would have gone up like a neglected still if you lit a match, but I never saw my father intoxicated, and I don't believe there was ever an hour in all the years he practiced medicine that he was incapacitated by alcohol. His attitude was that booze was a good icebreaker and destroyer of inhibitions, but beyond that a poison and a stealer of precious time. He resented the fact that liquor could make one sleepy in the acute phase, and later incapable of doing one's thing in the hangover stage. Time was too precious to him to risk losing any of it in an alcohol stupor. Consequently, he was very moderate in his imbibing, enjoying the flow and camaraderie induced by alcohol when taken in moderation, but saving his pagan indulgence for the food that accompanied it.

9

Cars

It was just prior to my birth that my father acquired his first automobile.[1] He had started his practice of medicine in Rutherford with a bicycle as his sole means of conveyance. Like all the young blades in his time he probably had been "checked out" in a horse-powered rig, but I don't think he ever qualified as a horse-and-buggy MD, except during his second summer of practice, 1912, when he substituted for a doctor on vacation. Anyway, 1913 to 1914 saw him at the wheel of his own Ford, and there began the classic man-auto duel that has been so often and so well told.[2]

Winter mornings meant kettles of hot water poured into the radiator, then setting the magneto and gas before starting the cranking ritual. Running from front bumper to the driver's seat to try to nurse that little spark of engine ignition before she stalled, and without flooding; skinning the knuckles; sweating to the point he had to come in the house and change his clothes down to the skin before starting out on his calls; cursing not just a little—all were part of the morning ritual. Then he covered the hood with a blanket when on a house call to preserve some heat to ease the next engine turn-over. At times being snowed in, when on an overnight maternity call, he did not even try to get started, but walked home and dug the car out later.Summertime it was easier to get going but there were more flats. Jack it up, pull off the shoe, peel out the tube, find the leak and patch it. Then pump. Always a bucket in the car for overheating, hauling water from the nearest horse trough, brook, spring, or bog.

And so it went, as Dad gradually worked up the scale in opulence, first from a Ford to a Dodge, and later, in 1917, to a Buick. Dad was never a car nut. A car was owned and maintained to serve its owner: Gas it, oil it, wash it, and when it wore out, get a new one. He was not his own mechanic. He trusted his serviceman and depended on him. No sentimentality about a car he owned.

When we boys were perhaps eight and ten years old in the middle 1920s, Dad had one of his Dodges which was just broken in and had had the 500-mile check-up. It had never been opened up wide and we were curious as to just how fast this machine could get over the ground. Five of us kids (Bill and Jim Black, Ick Platts, and my brother Paul and I) were packed onto the seats. Dad taxied her out West Passaic to Jackson Avenue and turned south down the river toward Newark. This was a speed trial, and we glued our eyes to the speedometer. Dad put the gas pedal to the floor, and somewhere between the Cooper Lumber Yard and the old Rutherford Avenue Bridge across the Passaic River we hit 45 miles an hour. He was as thrilled as we were. We yelled our approval and talked of it for weeks after.

Dad was no milquetoast on the road. Mom was continually imploring him, "Bill please slow down," or "Bill, please don't race that fool driver." Dad was a competitor, easily aroused by someone driving faster than he, or by someone showing the least sign of negligence or disrespect on the road. They had to be passed and put in their proper places. Coming down Route 17 on a Sunday night, returning from the farm in Monroe (Mom's folk's place) was a nightmare even in the twenties and thirties. Three or four hours to do the 45 miles. A suicidal trek down that three-lane slaughterhouse. Everyone tired and angry. Windows rolled down and fists shaking. Everyone fighting to get one car ahead. On these trips Dad was not detached and thinking beautiful thoughts to knock out on the typewriter at his next opportunity. No sir, he was right in there racing and cussing and fist shaking with the rest of them. Mom would be nervous and irritated, but we kids loved it and urged him on, if not vocally, at least in spirit.

I guess the nearest and dearest to his heart of all the cars he owned was a second-hand Buick, a two-door custom-built coupe that had enjoyed the blandishments of a rich old lady from Montclair for a couple of years before dad took over. It had less than 10,000 miles on it and was the biggest, loudest, and most powerful thing he had ever had on the road. A solid layer upon layer of baked paint finish, black, such as they were still putting on cars in the thirties was, believe me, a stinker to Simonize. Never could get it completely free of streaks. but Dad enjoyed warming it up, and then just racing her for a minute to hear her growl, but it was a bloody truck to drive when you got going over 50 and were on a round-topped Macadam road full of potholes And those shocks, wow! When you took her from Rutherford to Vermont or Buffalo, you had done a day's work.

But the most challenging auto experience of his life was the trip from West Haven, Connecticut, to Rutherford on the September day of the big hurricane in 1938. Dad had gone up to 201 Ocean Avenue to pick up his mother who always summered there in a cottage a few feet from the shore of Long Island Sound. The mass news media had not yet learned the art of precipitating general public hysteria at the approach of every major weather change. And who had a radio in the car to pick up bulletins? No weather forecaster had warned of the storm. I remember the day well because it was the opening day of my second year in medical college in New York City. The opening ceremonies were being conducted in the amphitheater on York Avenue, and because of the heat the tall windows on each side of the hall were opened to allow some ventilation. The winds accompanying the storm made such a moaning, whistling, and groaning in the openings that the windows were perforce closed to make the speakers audible. Our consequent discomfort was intense. The streets of Manhattan later than afternoon were littered with ruptured umbrellas, and quantities of signs blown off the faces of buildings.

And at about this same hour Dad started out that oyster-shell-paved drive from the cottage in West Haven, probably a little after noon. It was hot and windless. Little breakers from the sound were making their normal "slap-slushhhhhh" on the beach at the foot of the jumbled stone wall in front of the cottages. Things went well for the first hour or so, but as they came closer to the city, there began to be trees across the road, and heavy rain made the visibility a little sticky. Grounded power lines flashed and smoked where they shorted on the wet ground, and branches and leaves flew horizontally across the line of vision.

What do you do in the middle of a hurricane with an old lady almost 90 seated beside you, her impedimenta stacked about her? You just keep on going and hope for the best, which is just what they did. At every obstacle thrown or blown into their path they turned right or left, according to the possibility of the road. They saw practically no one. In one town Dad spoke to a policeman who had no constructive suggestions, so they kept going. Later he couldn't recall exactly which towns they passed through, but with cars all along their way pinned under trees, pulled off onto the shoulder, or otherwise rendered *hors-de-combat,* they somehow won through to the George Washington Bridge and home to Rutherford. Seven or eight hours to make what normally was a two- or three-hour trip. That evening he recounted to Mom that his mother, born and raised in the hurricane belt of the West Indies, had remarked at the height of the storm, "[w]hy, it's almost like a hurricane!"

Dad's cars played a big part in his trips with Mom. They took them off the beaten path—to places like Tapahannock on the Rapahanock one night where the girl in the restaurant apologized because all she could cook for them was fresh shad roe. Or on the run from Bangor to Island Falls up in Aroostook County, in the early twenties, absolutely everything was unpredictable, from the condition of the road to the availability of the next gasoline pump, food, and lodging. From Island Falls they drove across the Canadian border to smuggle back a few fifths of booze in the knickers that were the thing then for men out camping in Maine.

Dad was forever finding dandy stones for his path from the house to the garage, which stands today just as he finally completed it. Those stones were slung in the back of the car whenever and whenever they were found—at the farm in Monroe, on the shore at West Haven, at Garrett Mountain, at Cranberry Lake while visiting the Spences. And much of the landscaping of the property at 9 Ridge Road was done with trees and shrubs pulled up from spots as widely separated as the Cedar Swamps out in the Rutherford meadows and the Mohawk Trail in Massachusetts between Greenfield and North Adams. Hemlocks from three different states separate the back and side yards. Shad bushes from Great Notch, New Jersey, have done well, but the swamp azalea and blueberry bushes (which were doomed where they grew because of the ditching done by the mosquito commission to allow tide waters into the cedars) couldn't make it in our yard either.[3]

And there was devilry, too. Like the night the annual Williams, Spence, Wagner, and Dugdale progressive dinner was in motion from the Spence house at 23 Lincoln Avenue to our house on Ridge Road. It seemed appropriate to the New Year's Eve mood to deviate from the customary route and make a short cut on the sidewalk down Park Avenue along the west side of the Presbyterian Church. A member of the local constabulary interrupted the frolic about halfway down the block, but in keeping with the holiday mood, and on recognizing Dad, he advised him to get back on the road and wished him a Happy New Year. Similarly on another occasion, he drove in reverse from the Dugdale house on West Passaic to the Spences. The little thank-you-ma'am bridge on the Molly Stark Trail about a mile east of Wilmington up in Vermont seemed to invite Dad to charge it—this was a ritual we kids loved and anticipated with glee. The simple little arch over Beaver Brook when crossed at any speed over 30 miles an hour would toss the back wheels of the car up in the air like a bucking bronco, and of course we young ones would fly up and hit the roof over the rear seat. What fun!

And then there was Bobby. Dad had brought him home in his pocket one night, a gift from a patient whose bitch had spawned a litter of little mongrel terrier pubs. The one Dad pulled out from under the stove was a little white long-tailed male. We never had a sweeter pup. He was everyone's friend, from the sergeant on the desk at the police headquarters across the street on whom Bobby made a daily social call, to all the kids in the neighborhood who frequented our yard. Often Dad would leave in a hurry, jump into the car, and be off to a delivery or other urgent call. On arrival, there was Bobby, having somehow hung onto the running board all unbeknownst until discovered at their destination.

And at Hildale up in Vermont, driving over to Raponda for a swim on a summer's afternoon, Bobby would hop on the running board as we pulled away. This was a narrow dirt road with bushes growing close on both sides. The pup would take a beating from the wild cherry branches and blackberry stalks that slapped him as we went by. About every other trip the torture would get the best of him, and he'd look ahead for the next branch that was about to clip him and close his teeth on it. Of course, the car kept going, and unless Bobby let go promptly he was pulled off into the ditch, only to pick himself up on his front feet as the rolls and somersaults induced by the momentum of the car had ceased. Lost in the dust cloud behind the car, we could hear him better than we could see him as he tore along behind, yipping his head off.

10

Sports

Baseball

Dad enjoyed baseball as a player and as a spectator.[1] He pitched and played third. His brother Edgar was the catcher. In fact, Edgar played semi-pro summers in New England to bolster the exchequer while studying at Boston Tech. He was a good man with the bat. Carl Hubbell was Dad's hero, particularly his feat of striking out the American League's "murderers' row" in the All Star game of 1937. He also got a chuckle from the Giants's Jo-Jo Moore calmly reaching across the plate and stroking the ball to the left on a pitch intended for an intentional pass. Frankie Frisch was his favorite commentator of all the sports announcers. "Oh, those bases on balls."[2]

Dad's sensitivity and complete involvement in the game as player and/or spectator would manifest itself years later when he would be unable to sit and listen to, or watch on television, a tense situation. In the ninth inning with two out, score tied, bases jammed, and full count on the batter, he would have to excuse himself from the room and get the details later.

Tennis

Dad's involvement in tennis would be strictly hearsay were it not for letters he wrote to his brother Ed, who was in Rome for the Prix de Rome Fellowship, from July 17, 1911, when he told Ed he had joined the Rutherford Tennis Club, saying that he found it a "fine game and one in which I think I have a chance to become proficient."[3]

The following spring and summer he resumed playing tennis as a routine part of his daily life, and his game greatly improved. On June

21, 1912, he announced he was "making strides in my tennis and last Saturday managed to survive the first round of a handicap tournament for the first time." His next opponent forfeited through absence thus sending Williams "directly into the semi finals for a big silver cup."[4] Despite expecting he would lose, even with a handicap, he advanced to the finals, as the next letter of July 5, 1912, records. Whether he beat the previous year's champion and won the Tennis Club cup is not known, but he pronounced the challenge "[g]reat fun."[5]

Mom recalls a match in Paris in the early twenties on a neighborhood court in the vicinity of the residence of Ford Maddox Ford with Dad and Harold Loeb playing against Ford and Ernest Hemingway. Feelings ran high, because Loeb was Hemingway's financial crutch in those days, and furthermore had swiped Hemingway's girl, and Dad and "Hem" shared little other than their male attire and the purposeful juggling of words. Despite Hemingway's frequent interjections of "You have nothing" and "I'll wipe you off the court," neither team could win two successive games and end the match. Like so many amateurs, neither could break the other's service. The match ended with Hem quitting the court, complaining of his knee having given out.

Fencing

Dad and Edgar learned the basics of fencing while attending school in Paris. He kept up with this sport at the University of Pennsylvania where he fenced on the Varsity team.

Returning to Rutherford to practice medicine, he occasionally had the opportunity to go to a club in New York City with a couple of local buffs of the sword. I can recall his canvas suit and the headpiece with the wire visor which he would on occasion don, perhaps for my amusement, pantomiming the feints and lunges of combat on the old mat in the attic. Two of his foils are still there, gathering dust in a corner. Although I was taken along to watch the workouts at the club in the city, I was not really enchanted, and never got the urge to participate. My idea of dueling was Doug Fairbanks in *Robin Hood* or *The Black Pirate.* These middle-aged civilians in dueling garb, dancing back and forth on the narrow strip of matting, shouting in French, filling the air with metallic scapings and crashes, and finally admitting to being stabbed by shouting "touché," just never turned me on.

Fishing

The killer sports never interested Dad. While I knew him he never owned a gun or fishing rod, though in his youth he used handmade fishing poles or borrowed Pa Herman's rods. Paul and I, on the other hand, have always been avid fishermen.[6] On occasion Dad would accompany us, particularly when we went to the point east of the cottage at West Haven on Long Island Sound, fishing for conners and blacks off the rocks, or dunking speering under bobbers attached to long bamboo poles when the snapper blues were running off Woodmont. I guess his kicks came from being with us boys and sharing in our triumph with each catch.

On the last day of summer camp (Camp Roosevelt, near Island Falls, Maine) on Lake Mattawamkeag in August 1924, a fellow Rutherfordian camper lacked a fifth variety of fish to complete his qualifications for his camp letter. Jack Holbrook was a little bigger and older than I, one of my heroes I guess, and I enticed Dad to row us out to Devil's Wall. This was a jagged ridge of rock that jutted above the surface a couple of miles down the lake. It was a bass paradise, with weed beds each side of the wall ending at a sharp drop-off into deep water. Any kid could catch a bass on practically every cast. In fact, Bill Sewell used to take groups of parents lodged in his cabins down there in his motorboat. Hell, even our mothers caught bass. But not Jack. Dad rowed us down there, made a couple of loops around Devil's Wall, and then rowed back to camp. Jack had sat tensely gripping his rod, refusing all my advice about changing lures, checking for weeds on the hook, etc. He caught nothing.

When we beached the boat, next to the bateau in front of the camp, Jack disconsolately reeled in his line. As the lure came to the side of the boat there hove into view a big blob of weeds. Dejectedly Jack started to clean the mess off the hooks, when lo and behold in the center of the weeds appeared a bass. Barely ten inches long (the required size to qualify), drowned like a pickle in a barrel, it had been dragged for God knows how many miles. We were all ecstatic, and Jack got his letter.

I recall a late September day with half a gale blowing and white caps making the water off the beach at Oyster River a solid blanket of foam. At my insistence Dad and I ventured out in a flat-bottomed rowboat. The tide was coming in, I had a bucket of clams and a rod, the sky was gray, and we were closing the cottage for the season. Dad pulled that leaking, unmanageable tub back and forth across the mouth of the river a dozen times, the two of us bracing our bare feet on the opposing seats, licking the spray off our lips, the brine running in rivulets off our chins and elbows, and puddling on the seats beneath us. To a fisherman it was heaven, and to Dad at the oars it was a challenge

Crabs stole the bait, weeds weighted the line. It became a comedy of frustration. We agreed on a last pass across the river's mouth. I like to think it was a lunker striper. We never saw him. The rod tip was under water, the mid-section of the rod ratatattatting on the gunwale. I instinctively jumped up and reared back. Thud, thud, thud. Three magnificent heaves on the line and he was gone. I toppled over backwards, flattening Dad. The two of us, with oars on top, tangled in the bow with the remainder of my gear.

11

Gardening

There was a daily ritual arm-in-arm circuit of the yard, usually early in the morning before leaving for the hospital, as he and mother inspected and planned the plantings. They shared a love of growing things, and from the appearance of the first snowdrop in late February until the last mums and wild asters gave up the ghost in late November, the garden was a major item of activity and conversation at our home. There was always a wet newspaper or burlap-wrapped bundle of wild things in the car when he and mother returned from a trip. Ferns, moss, wild orchid, ginger, trillium, wild violets in variety, trailing arbutus, wild geranium were healed into a protected spot until my parents could decide just where in the yard they would be most likely to survive.

He knew and enjoyed the use of outdoor tools. Snapshots in the family album show him down in a hole in the backyard chopping the roots of a massive oak stump. This was in 1916, with me in my white play suit equally involved in moving dirt. He made all the foundation plantings in front of 9 Ridge Road, and he and Mom together constructed a 300 square-foot rock garden along the north wall of the house. He double dug and planted a half-dozen rose beds in the backyard over the years, the final one remaining to this day and blooming in season. At the Hermans' (Mom's parents) farm in Monroe, New York, he did haying, gardening, and road repairs, and later, with me and Paul, built a dam down in the woods to create a pond that would attract wildlife. At Hilldale, at Mom's Uncle Einar's place in Wilmington, Vermont, he used a scythe to cut the millet that was fed to the cows each evening in the summer months. Up there he shared in the annual chore of burying the rocks that heaved up in the lane from the main road every spring. And the cutting of wood with a two-man saw, wedges, and splitting axe was a daily routine at both farms.

He knew the smaller hand tools as well, having been indoctrinated in carpentry by his father, who was an able craftsman in the shop. Rake, hoe, saw, scythe, pickaxe, sledgehammer, clippers, mower, he used them all knowledgeably, but I think the shovel family was his favorite. The gardening fork and spade were his constant companions in the yard when making his rounds. He definitely related to dirt. With a fork one can dig it, move it, aerate it, cultivate it, or scarify it. And all these things he did, while I was growing up, in an old pair of Oxfords, sleeveless undershirt, and his other companion, the old fedora.

In the 1940s, with Dad in his sixties, there began a friendship with Professor Charles Abbott at the University of Buffalo. How this came about I am not sure; probably it was initiated by Charles and fostered by Dad through a sense of appreciation for the attention, a kind of TLC.[1]

I first drove the folks up there in the spring of 1946, and they stayed on for a couple of weeks as the guests of Charles and Theresa on the Gratwick estate near Pavilion or Linwood, New York, well south of Buffalo. It is an idyllic site, 350 acres on a ridge sloping south and east, the land partly wooded and the rest largely cultivated and pasture.[2] It was obviously a wealthy man's country abode, with a central manor house and, scattered about, several satellite residences which had once housed the farmer, coachman, butler, etc. In the postwar, post–Depression times of the forties, maintenance of house and grounds wasn't quite up to Gratwick standards. But the evidence of former glory was everywhere, in the walled garden with the espaliered fruit trees; the sunken garden with the central lily pond, and surrounding wall of elms; the Venetian garden with the canaliculi dividing the flower beds; the two swimming pools, tennis court, greenhouse, stables, and pond, carriage museum, all joined by a maze of paths and roadways surrounding and mostly leading eventually to the central manor house. All formality of design and borders was lost to the encroaching weeds and brush that had insinuated their way into the plantings. Woodchucks burrowed, feasted, bred, and reproduced prolifically in the jungle, and what remained of the lawns was well fertilized and close cropped by wandering sheep.

Centrally located but lost in the herbage was a small stone chapel with multifaceted walls fenestrated by narrow, unglazed windows starting at head height and extending up into the gloom overhead. A small lectern, niches in the walls for candle holders, a few hymnals, and a couple of scone benches completed the furnishings. Capacity about 12. The services, conducted by the authors. The folks occupied an apartment over the stables near the main gate, neighboring the house of the Abbotts, which, as I recall, had once been the residence of one of the leading functionaries on the place. Here Mom could prepare breakfast, served at a table overlooking the hen yard, where an old gander ruled the roost, trumpeting and honking at man or beast with the temerity to trespass on or near his domain.

The surrounding hedge abounded with birds, robins nesting, catbirds, warblers, cardinals, sparrows, and the chatterbox wrens, and beyond was Charles Abbott's vegetable garden, precisely planted and immaculately maintained. Fresh herbs, salad greens, cherry tomatoes, berries, and tender young root crops, all less than a stone's throw from the kitchen door, planted in an elongated oval, framing a central patch of grass. This was one of Charles' *sancta*, which I quite innocently defiled one warm hazy morning by weeding and cultivating thoroughly from end to end, supposing all the while that I not only was getting a workout and a tan but was doing Charles a helluva favor. Unfortunately, this was a Gratwick Farm no-no. *Verboten*! *Defendu*! No one, but no one, touched Charles's garden. So when he returned from Buffalo that evening, I was well off in the fields with my rifle, potting woodchucks. Fortunately, I am a bit of a garden buff myself, and if I do say so, I'd done a damn good job! And Charles did the sporting thing, not only forgiving me my trespasses after his inspection found no damage done, but granting me license thereafter to have at his precious garden when, if, and as the urge should strike me.

To the west of the Abbott house was an old tumbled-down greenhouse and pigeon loft, where Bill Gratwick conducted his tree peony culture. He of course was owner, boss, manager, and resident factotum of his peony business, which at that time was in its formative years. The greenhouse benches held the grafted seedlings which had been painstakingly bred in the field rows of wild Chinese tree peony stock. Pollination of the peonies was accomplished early on a windless morning at a time when the field plants were full of maturing but unopened peony buds. The green bud is carefully peeled open to reveal the reproductive parts, specifically the pistil, which is then fertilized with the pollen of some distinguished blossom the characteristics of which the nurseryman wishes to perpetuate, the pollen having been previously collected from ripe flowers into papers folded snuggly against chance pollen particles wind-borne in the air. This one accomplishes by dipping a camel's-hair brush in the pollen, transferring it to the female organ. The bud is then closed and further shielded by applying a covering bag which is tied over the bud and the terminal stem with twine. This ritual Dad and I shared in and saw the benches full of the resulting potted grafts developing toward the day when it would be apparent from the flower whether the whole procedure had been worthwhile. And so Dad's involvement in the growing led to his becoming the Poet Laureate of the Tree Peonies, riding to the sunken garden on a tractor, in the absence of a chariot, and there receiving the honorary award from Harriet Gratwick.

The developing embryonic forms of the young peony plants are a fit subject and challenge for the artist. The tender, waxy cotyledons, peeling in sensuous whorls from the central phallus, and the system of divisions to form branches, suggest the parts of bodies in intimate embrace. Bill Gratwick sculpted the spirit of the goddess hidden among the curving leaves, and the Greek painter Nassos Daphnis, in summer residence from New York City, did the same in his own medium. Daphnis was Gratwick's partner in the hybridizing program, and he gave his hybrids the names of Greek goddesses. It was Dad's challenge to capture in words this process of creation, from the moment of conception to the final divine fruition:

From THE YELLOW TREE PEONY (1946)

The girl whose arms are leaves
at whose heart
a small flower with
bowed head
hides its moon-glow
of remote thought—[3]

12

Girls

Man's relationship to any members of the sexes, be they anatomically male or female, is a very subjective thing, as my father has suggested in his *Autobiography.* And what can a firstborn son tell of his parents' sexual orientation and motivation, other than to observe modifications of the parents' behavior in sexually stimulating situations. Furthermore, who is to say what experience is stimulating, what turns him on? He has said in his *Autobiography,* "I am extremely sexual in my desires," yet "[w]hat relations I have had with men and women, such encounters as have interested me most profoundly, have not occurred in bed."[1] One is forced to wonder about the spectrum of experience which is included in his definition of sexual desires. "I was an innocent sort of child and have remained so to this day,"[2] he writes as he approaches 70 years of age.

Innocent indeed! Childhood experiences that may be interpreted as "sexual" include watching a young woman take a bath from a basin as she stands nude, he watching through a knothole; and observing his grandmother dress while a quilt with a peephole is draped over his head.[3] His was a sheltered childhood in an ethically proper Unitarian household.[4] Other than yellow journalism there was no miasma of sexually explicit garbage such as our modern media exploit. As a reflection of the community attitude toward "dirt," he would be sent home from grade school, the Sylvan School, by Principal Helen Walcott when he was found to have on his person a collection of cards (distributed in cigarette packs) revealing naughty chorus girls in bloomers. He could return to school only if accompanied by his mother.

As a youngster he would dangle and entangle bare legs while ostensibly fishing off a dock with a young sweetheart. This moment he remembers as one in which "the sun and clouds meeting over our heads did a seraphic *pas de deux*, so that I thought the world a paradise."[5] However, he continues, "I burned her letters to me during my first year at Penn—the final act before the next phase."

Alors. Young Lochinvar prances off into manhood, his virginal white burgee born high on his lance, signifying his inherent, instinctive, primordial masculinity, unconditioned by carnal stimuli. No armor, no shield to rend off the advances and blandishments of the opposite sex. An aura of naivete, a palpable cloud of innocence went with him, but aura and cloud would be permeated with the pure essence of male soma. No need for ogling, muscle flexing, breath sweeteners, hot-dogging in general. No need to advertise. The Real McCoy sells itself.

And a very important phase it would be. In the freshman dorms he met Ezra Pound and began a stormy friendship that would last a lifetime. In addition to the cultural stimulation that Ezra supplied, two women, Hilda Doolittle and Viola Baxter Jordan, provided exposure to a facet of life, man-woman interplay on an adult level, that heretofore he had not experienced.

Hilda Doolittle

At the Pound residence in Wyncote in April 1905, Dad met Hilda Doolittle, and thereafter he would frequently take the cross-country trolley to Upper Darby to visit Hilda, sometimes with Ezra, sometimes not. Apparently she found Billy Williams quite sympathetic to her interest in poetry without being domineering and professorial like the young Ezra. They took long walks together, enjoying the beauties of nature (grape hyacinths and hepaticas), and on one occasion weathering a rainstorm, at her insistence, out in an open field. He took her to a Mask and Wig trying out dance, drawing dirty looks from Pound over it. He slept over at the Doolittle house one night in a borrowed nightgown from Hilda's father, the old professor of astronomy. From my father's *Autobiography*:

> Hilda, tall, blond and with a long jaw but gay blue eyes was, I think, much like her father [...].
>
> There was about her that which is found in wild animals at times, a breathless impatience, almost a silly unwillingness to come to the point. She

had a young girl's giggle and shrug which somehow in one so tall and angular seemed a little absurd. She fascinated me, not for her beauty, which was unquestioned if bizarre to my sense, but for a provocative indifference to rule and order which I liked. She dressed indifferently, almost sloppily and looked to a young man not inviting—she had nothing of that—bur irritating, with a smile.

Ezra was wonderfully in love with her and I thought exaggerated her beauty ridiculously. To me she was just a good guy and I enjoyed, uncomfortably, being with her.[6]

Her self-image as a young woman, as she describes herself years later while undergoing analysis with Sigmund Freud, reinforces my father's concept of indeterminate sex:

[A] girl between two boys, but, ironically, it was wispy and mousey, while the boys [her brothers] were glowing and golden. It was not pretty, they said. Then they said it was pretty—but suddenly, it shot up like a weed. They said, surprised, "She is really very pretty, but isn't it a pity she's so tall."[7]

Note the repetition of the neuter "it."

Perhaps she really didn't turn on his sexual drive, although Dad's first praise of her in a letter to his brother Ed, or "Bo," dated Wednesday, April 12, 1905, after the dinner party hosted by Pound, says she is "all to the mustard":

He had five fellows for supper and five girls and at last I have met some classy ladies. They're a deuced of an intellectual bunch, daughters of professors, doctors, etc., but they are fine. Not one is good looking, I mean pretty, but they are all pleasant to look upon because they are so nice. One in particular struck me. She is tall, about as tall as I am, young, about eighteen and, well, not round and willowy, but rather bony, no that doesn't express it, just a little clumsy but all to the mustard She is a girl that's full of fun, bright, but never telling you all she knows, doesn't care if her hair is a little mussed, and wears good solid shoes. She is frank and loves music and flowers, and I got along with her pretty well.[8]

Hilda invited everyone to a party at her house the following Saturday, and Billy told his brother:

We got to her house at three o'clock and found a party, we included, of eight girls and eight fellows all in their old clothes. [...].

Anyway we went despising road and paths, right across fields on the run, just like a game of hare & hounds [...] till every one simply had to get into the game. Well this lasted hours then Miss Doolittle, that's her name, found

> some flowers and got down beside them to protect them from the rest of the party. I sat down beside her and the rest passed on. We began talking of flowers when she said she knew a place where hepaticas grew so thick the ground was blue with them. I said I would like to see it and we being at the tail end of the crowd turned aside and had a great two hours walk by ourselves. Oh Bo but she is a fine girl, no simple nonsense about her no false modesty and all that, she is absolutely free and innocent. We talked of the finest things: of Shakespeare, of flowers, trees, books, & pictures. [...] She said I was Rosalind in As You Like It and she was Celia, so I called her that although her name is Hilda.
>
> The evening was spent at the house of another of the girls who lives out in the country also. We had a great time singing and dancing and, by the way, I have a reputation as a songster which is rapidly spreading. I got home at twelve, covered with some mud, a little glory and oceans of a fine comfortable happy feeling inside of me somewhere. I am going to call some day, perhaps.[9]

Yet a year and a half later, November 12, 1906, Bill announced the following to Edgar:

> To do what I mean to do and to be what I must be in order to satisfy my own self I must discipline my affections and until a fit opportunity affords like no one in particular except you Bo and my nearest family. From nature Bo I have a weakness wherever passion is concerned. No matter how well I may reason and no matter how clearly I can see terrible results of yielding up to desire if certain conditions are present I might as well never have arrived at a consecutive conclusion for good in all my life for I cannot control myself. As a result, in order to preserve myself as I must girls cannot be my friends.[10]

On one occasion on arrival at the Pound house, Ezra challenged Dad to a friendly duel with two of his father's walking sticks. As Dad took the *en garde* position, Ezra came charging in and caught him just above the right eye. Dad threw down his stick in disgust and quit the field of battle. Had Dad's attentions to H.D. aroused the green-eyed monster, jealousy, in friend Ezra? It does seem reasonable.

The final get-together of the gang from Penn and Upper Darby in June 1906 almost ended in tragedy as Hilda impulsively rushed into rough surf at Point Pleasant, New Jersey, and was dragged out unconscious by Bob Lamberton, a friend whom Dad described as "a tough tackle on the Varsity,"[11] and who is pictured in the UPenn yearbook as a Varsity swimmer. However, she was resuscitated, and, apparently, feeling none the worse for the experience, finished our day canoeing on the Manasquan River as the gang "sang our farewell songs to each other."[12] They never met as a group again. Ezra Pound was not present, having already left for Spain for research on his doctoral dissertation.

Dad went on to New York for his internship at French Hospital. And it was while interning that he received a postcard addressed to him there, postmarked Upper Darby, Pennsylvania, September 18, 1907. On the card a photo of the Manasquan River from Pine Buff Inn, Point Pleasant, and the message saying,

> Dear Billy—
>
> I have just returned.
> Sorry you scorned us.
> We had a dandy time. H.

In September 1907, Pound was teaching French and Spanish at Wabash College in Crawfordsville, Indiana. By 1908, Pound was in London and meeting with some success in getting his work published. Dad had a letter from him suggesting he follow suit and "come across & broaden your mind."[13] Dad visited him in London in early 1910, on his way home after Leipzig, and later that year Ezra also returned home, for several months, visiting Rutherford frequently and staying at the Williams house on West Passaic Avenue during Thanksgiving. Hilda was visiting also, as recorded on November 28, 1910, in a letter to brother Ed: "Pound and Hilda Doolittle spent two or twenty days here a short time ago, I'm pretty sure it was only two. They are geniuses but wearying, they would say bewildering." Soon thereafter, in 1911, Hilda would write to Billy to say she was going to England, presumably to join Pound, her fiancé. My father describes his farewell to her: "I went down to the dock to bid her goodbye and found her sitting on a trunk, her father, the old astronomer, beside her, uncommunicative as always. I doubt that he even saw me. It was a disconsolate picture."[14]

H.D. next appeared in the life of my father in 1920 in New York City, in company with her companion Bryher. She had informed him she was coming to New York en route to Los Angeles where the two women intended to make their home, and wouldn't he like to drop in on them at the Belmont Hotel some afternoon for tea? Invitation accepted, Dad took along Bob McAlmon, and it was there that Bryher (Miss Annie

Winifred Ellerman) first laid eyes on her soon-to-be husband. In reply to Dad's asking Bob his opinion of H.D., he replied, "'[o]h, she's all right, I guess,' said Bob. 'But that other one, Bryher, as she was introduced to us—she's something.'"[15] The other one is described by WCW as "a small, dark English girl, with piercing, intense eyes." Thus was born the "normalization" of Miss Ellerman as a married woman (Bryher McAlmon), apparently to insure continuation of financial support from her shipping magnate papa. There was also some question whether the old boy's largesse would continue in the face of the lesbian "marriage" of his daughter Bryher to H.D. The unconsummated legal marriage of Bryher and Bob McAlmon would thus serve to remove the stigma of the relationship with Hilda Aldington.

The intimate dinner after the wedding featured the orchids provided by Dad's friend Edward ("Rudy") Roehrs, the famed nurseryman of East Rutherford, New Jersey. Mom had suggested orchids as appropriate for a couple who had everything, and Mr. Roehrs, with Dad looking on, had obligingly stripped his orchid house of all its blooms and packed them in a long carton. When displayed at the dinner they had inspired Marsden Hartley to suggest a newspaper headline of "POETS PAWING ORCHIDS!"[16] This was entirely appropriate, since most of the guests were poets: McAlmon, Marianne Moore, H.D., Bryher, Williams, and Hartley. Several days later Dad received a card signed "D.H.," with a "scene from some hit then playing showing several actors, men and women with their hands in a pot of money." He later accused H.D. of being the sender and would never believe her denial.

It was a most unsettling and bewildering experience for Bill to have Hilda, the chum of his young manhood, enmeshed in an uncomfortable *ménage à trois* with his recently acquired disciple, Bob McAlmon. She, since their last get-together, had suffered a series of tragedies, including the loss of her first child, the failure of her marriage to Richard Aldington, and the death of her father right after her brother Gilbert died in World War I. She chose not to stay with the father of her daughter Perdita. What had ostensibly started as a trip to England to meet her supposed fiancé, Ezra Pound, had become a financial, social, and psychological impasse, from which she was rescued by the adoring Bryher, who whisked her off to Greece, nursed her back to health, and from that time forward sought to be her crutch, her support both emotional and financial. McAlmon, with the suddenly acquired wealth of his marriage to Bryher, joined the artists' colony of Americans in Europe, and thus the Ellerman fortune helped to finance the publishing of their books, which included Dad's *Spring and All* and *The Great American Novel*, Pound's *Indiscretions; or, Une Revue de Deux Mondes*, and Hemingway's *In Our Time*.

As a six or seven-year-old boy, I can recall McAlmon visiting 9 Ridge Road, wearing a tanned leather vest, which Paul and I very much admired, and which he removed and left with us. On the same visit, I remember his whipping a primitive East African spear from the front hall into the molding at the base of a window in the living room—the scar remains in the molding to this day. Following an afternoon I had spent in a corner under the eaves of a poets' rendezvous somewhere in the village (pacified with a navel orange, which I slowly peeled, dissected, and ingested), Dad was dropping Bob at his current sleeping place, and as he slammed the door he, McAlmon, remarked to Dad, "[I]f you see Marianne, tell her I wouldn't throw her out of bed." In retrospect I must have been seven, because a six-year-old certainly wouldn't have understood the connotation. This would have occurred before McAlmon married Bryher in 1921.

McAlmon's particular inferno in Europe, he confessed to my parents, included, according to Dad's *Autobiography*, "long train trips about the continent with the two women quarreling in the compartment driving him nearly insane," adding "hard to go on like that."[17] He remained a good friend to both Bill and Flossie, "a live one," as they said. He spent much time with them on their trip abroad in 1924. And Flossie would remark in a letter from Paris in 1927 to her husband:

> Glad you had a nice letter from Bob [McAlmon]. You and he should be friends and I hope you feel so toward him. I like him and enjoy being with him—I am with him as you say you are with Madeline—not constrained.

Viola Baxter Jordan

While the four-and-a-half-year-old Billy Williams was being placed outside the house on Passaic Avenue after the legendary blizzard of March 1888, a little nymph, nicknamed "Billy" Baxter, was celebrating her first birthday on March 15 in Utica, New York. William Carlos Williams yelled to be taken back inside the shelter of his home, away from the 50-foot-high snowdrifts and the cold winds. There is no record of what the infant in Utica, Viola Baxter Jordan, was experiencing on that memorable day. We do know that about 20 years later these two met at 143 East 83rd Street through the auspices of their mutual friend, Ezra Pound, who had written a letter of introduction to the interning Dr. Williams, promising to provide him with her address. And the young medico in turn would write to his confidante, brother Edgar: "I received a letter from Ezra Pound today in which he introduces me to a most excellent New York girl. I am going to see her soon."[18] Pound had met her in 1905 at a dance while he was a student at Hamilton College.

The experience of the blizzard was frightening, awesome, an unforgettable childhood event. Viola on the other hand would prove an enchanting Venus, a titillating prize pursued for the rest of his life and never attained. She had completed her education in evening high school in Utica, enrolling in courses in typing and shorthand, and attained some competence in German, Italian, and French, her goal being to become an opera singer. When her parents divorced, she came to New York with her mother and found employment as a secretary at Oxford University Press, but also became a "super" or supernumerary at the Metropolitan Opera, doing walk-ons and singing in the chorus. She recorded in her diary, read courtesy of her daughter, Barbara, that Enrico Caruso whispered to her in Italian, "[y]ou have beautiful eyes." The observation was fortified by the German baritone Otto Goritz in English, and years later by her husband Virgil D. Baxter, who would describe them as "brown bees that sting."

She also had aspirations to write, stimulated no doubt by lifelong correspondence with three established pen pushers, Pound, Williams, and Doolittle. Their style was not to her taste, as she repeatedly emphasized in her letters. Her daughter Barbara also responded to my questions about Viola's disapproval of aspects of their writing: "Yes, yes, yes! Many were the books with her vehement 'bosh!!' in margins [...] complete with exclamatory points!" However, she was a marvelous and generous correspondent, composing long, chatty letters to Pound, mildly sexy, teasing letters to Bill, and gossipy, consoling ones to Hilda. When Pound was in St. Elizabeths Hospital, she sent him many packages of food and other gifts.[19]

For 50 years these two dynamic people, Viola and Bill, would communicate in one way or another, two vibrant people with receptors extended in all directions. When together, they hovered like butterflies over a flower bed on a hot summer day, stimulated by the colors and odors, energized by the heat, touching wings and antennae sporadically, parting and returning to their random sampling of the feast spread out below them. Each was catalyst for the other, their performance intensified and magnified in the other's presence. Their meetings and correspondence were not necessarily of world-shaking significance, but to them they were sufficiently memorable to be recalled and recorded, she in her diary, he in his *Autobiography*.

The Siren Viola was a strong voice in the chorus of stimuli that influenced Williams for many years. Even as he was courting Floss, the minx in New York was foremost in his dreaming. Having established his formal engagement to Flossie, and shipped off to Germany for some postgraduate studies, he continued to correspond with Viola.

> Leipzig of course! Naturally
> Emilienstr. 34
> Jan. 23, 1910
>
> Dear Viola: There is something magical about you and yet not entirely fairy like. It riles me and, frankly, makes me think more of imps than angels, but even here you have no exact counterpart.
>
> [...] I am in Germany; "how peculiar," you say, and trying to study, again you remark, this time, "how unusual," but it remains a fact even if you don't agree with Darwin's *Descent of Man*. Wasn't that the book?
>
> [...] These people [Germans] have the spontaneity of a freight train, and although much that they accomplish is altogether necessary and worthwhile, the greater part of their beauty is of the theoretically correct variety which is bred only by a crass, unsympathetic egotism.
>
> You see, I do not like Germans, and yet I must admire them, [...].[20]

In view of his later admiration and love for, and alliance with, his German father-in-law Paul Herman, who was unjustly suspected of treasonous activity during World War I, the last two sentences are an interesting observation.

The relationship was only briefly interrupted by his marriage in 1912. But the mood of their friendship was tempered by his marriage to Flossie, though there had never been any greater intimacy than a kiss, which Viola would report to Pound had occurred "at his suggestion on the corner of a street years ago!!!" In an earlier letter she had told Pound: "Funny I never had a lover—I can't really be bothered."

Viola married Virgil Jordan in 1914, two years after my Mom and Dad's ceremony. The distaste Viola felt for Floss, and probably Floss for her, was gradually dissipated over the years to the extent that there was a social intercourse between two households. From Viola's diary, 1918:

> Bill and Florence came over about 6 and asked us to go to the "Blue Bird" for supper as Bill had made some extra money on the influenza epidemic and said he had had a little party with two maidens while she [Floss] was at Idylease, convalescing from influenza, so could stand one for her [...]. [N]o drinks served on Sunday, so we had oysters and lovely ones, steak and mushrooms, chocolate cake and coffee. Bill spoke French with the waiter [...].

On December 11, 1918, she wrote in her diary about a musical evening out with Bill and Flossie and the Jordan children, Susan and Barbara: "Went to hear Yvette Guilbert!! Bill took us as far as Hackensack in car at midnight [...] a short ride but quite wearisome on trolley. I said goodbye and kissed my hand to his nose and he said goodbye dearest."

The Baroness

In a letter to Dad dated January 11, 1928, Flossie writes: "I might just as well tell you not to send me letters from people like this Pauline Leader, who sounds to me like another Evelyn Scott or Baroness—they both started in about the same fashion and were damn nuisances before you got rid of them. But no doubt you'll deplore my lack of literary values so there you are."

Around 1920, while dragging the boondocks for talent for his publications, Dad admired a piece of sculpture in the apartment of Margaret Anderson and Jane Heap in New York City. In his own words, this masterpiece "appeared to be chicken guts."[21] It was identified as the work of an artist named Elsa von Freytag-Loringhoven, a Baroness and an émigré from Germany, who became an active participant in the Dada movement in New York. Dad admired her work and expressed a wish to meet the artist, who, incidentally, was "crazy" about the work of William Carlos Williams.

Dada, according to the *Merriam Webster Dictionary*, was "an artistic movement based on deliberate irrationality and negation of the laws of beauty and organization." This the Baroness demonstrated flagrantly both in her art and in her dress and behavior. Her costumes included a bra consisting of two tomato cans secured with a string tie behind, and a coal scuttle or a peach basket for a hat. Or she paraded her almost nude body through Greenwich Village clad in a "black Mother Hubbard with moons cut out front and back for ready reference."[22]

Through mutual friends in the arts, a meeting of the Baroness with Williams was tentatively arranged. However, the lady had been temporarily ensconced in jail for stealing an umbrella. Dad had to bail her out on the day of her release, and after paying her bail, took her to breakfast. She turned out to be a dirty, bedraggled specimen of womanhood with a strong German accent, perhaps beautiful once. Dad called on her one day in the slum room where she lived: "We talked well and I was moved. But when later she went into her act, I put up a fight."[23] It seems it was her wish to give Dad syphilis so that he might free his mind for serious art.

The fascination the Baroness conceived for Dad was very serious. On two occasions she came to Rutherford. The first time she had an accomplice call the house on a bogus emergency involving a sick baby. Dad grabbed his bag and went out to his car, where she waylaid him demanding, "[y]ou must come with me."[24] He resisted and she "hauled off and hit me alongside the neck with all her strength."[25] A passing policeman offered to intervene, but Dad said to let her go. However, he purchased a punching bag "to take it out on in the cellar," and when she next attacked him on Park Avenue in Rutherford one evening a few months later, he "flattened her with a stiff punch to the mouth," had her arrested and jailed, but had her set free when she promised never to do it again.[26] He later gave her 200 dollars to get out of the country, which was stolen by a go-between. He gave her more cash, and she finally left, "only to be playfully killed by some French jokester, it is said, who turned the gas jet on in her room while she was sleeping."[27]

Nurses and Patients

As a young intern at French Hospital in New York, prepping in the scrub room alongside a young French nun, he noticed that

> her torso from the waist up was tightly held in a starched bodice which fitted her to perfection. Big dark eyes, full lips, and she said to me one day in excellent English, "Doctor Williams, if I were not a Sister, I would marry you."

Then she laughed.

"Well," I said, "if you were not a Sister...." And I laughed too.[28]

And during the same period of service he would be cornered in the pharmacy by the night supervisor, this little plea for intimacy terminating in a sterile assignation in a little room under the eaves on West 23rd Street.[29]

In his Rutherford office, in all his years of office hours, seeing primarily women and their children, he worked solo, never feeling the need for nursing or secretarial assistance. On occasion Floss was summoned to stand by while a pelvic exam was conducted, but otherwise his was a strictly one-on-one practice. This intimate privacy provided opportunity for some of his lady friends to seek a relationship ordinarily not included in the usual office visit. I recall a letter to Floss when she was in Switzerland, and Dad alone here in the States, describing an episode in the office, the woman begging for sexual intimacy, and he hard pressed to make it understood that he was a married man and really not interested. And on another occasion a patient, who was also a family friend, being the last patient of the evening, cornered him in his laboratory alcove and poured out her passion for him. She recently told me of his response: "Dear E ... , it's too late."

A large part of his professional life was spent at the Passaic General Hospital, where he was in attendance almost daily making the rounds of his patients, delivering babies, seeing clinic patients, attending committee meetings and clinicopathological conferences.[30] He was also involved in the teaching of nursing students, many of whom stayed on at the hospital after graduation and became long-time friends. He was fondly known to these girls as "Uncle Billy," and Marie Leone, a long-time head nurse in charge of clinics, tells me this nickname gives a good idea of his presence at the hospital. He was not an ass-pincher or a letch making suggestions for assignations. An arm around the waist and a friendly squeeze were the limits of his approach while on the job. Yet when a student complained that she didn't understand some of his poetry and asked for an explanation of a particular title, he said, "if I am going to explain this poem, we will have to have a table between us."

Of quite another caliber was Annie Oley, another of his girls, a real wheel horse who for many years ran the newborn nursery. Industrious, strong, and faithful, a maiden lady to her death, she would demonstrate her emotional lability with a red suffusion from hairline to bra top when praised or teased. She it was who became Dad's repository for numerous bits of verse written in odd moments on the road or in the delivery room. "Keep this for me, Annie." Reportedly, there developed quite a file of material, which unfortunately was lost when Annie's mother died and she moved to new quarters.[31]

In early 1948, Dad suffered the first of a series of vascular accidents, this one myocardial, which necessitated bed rest at home for a protracted period, and brought many gifts from the girls at Passaic General Hospital. Perhaps his letter of thanks will best reveal the type of warm, earthy relationship he enjoyed with the nurses:

March 3, 1948

Dear Girls:

I won't say "I don't know how to thank you" for that over whelming "shower" of gifts and good wishes—and names!!!—for I do know how to thank you: I'll tell you all about it.

But I've got to start with the razor—I could tell you a story about *that*—how one of my big sons took mine to be adjusted and left it in a subway station—but no more of that. I needed a new razor badly and this is a beauty. Why it's so good I cut my lip with it shaving in bed this morning. Some of the aptness in such a gift comes to, I suppose, that I had such a close shave with this old pump of mine last month. I also love the light tan pajamas (God knows I need them too) "they go so well with your eyes" as my sweet community nurse told me this morning—pretty soft, huh? Boy! Can she rub my back! And you ought to see her get on the back rung of my hospital bed (from the Red Cross), lean over me, grab the mattress on both sides and yank it up toward the head of the bed! Wow! She's got umpf, she has. She learned it in the army!

They won't let me into the bathroom so I can't play with my water toys—but I've got a beautiful commode and do I look handsome sitting on it, you'd be surprised!

But I'm saving the chocolate apple for later and the books too for the day when I finally get through reading Sigmund Freud's *The Interpretation of Dreams*. That is a tough one, but I enjoy it tremendously and warmly recommend it to you—but not until after you're married or something, take it from me, and have I had *dreams*, lying here in bed. I couldn't possibly tell you. Such dreams! Such lovely dirty dreams.

Well that leaves only the baby to account for. She's a honey—if I only knew who her *mother* is, bless 'er 'eart.

And that's enough for tonight as I'm beginning to get a little tired. I'll keep you posted as to my progress, count on that.

I will surely let you hear from me again at the end of this week.

Love,

Uncle Bill

Nurses encountering Doc Williams at hospitals other than the Passaic, could not believe that he was a poet. Donald Cox, who was born in Rutherford, and grew up there, remembers:

> When Dr. Williams visited patients at Hackensack Hospital, my sister, a nurse there, would point him out to her fellow nurses as a poet. They could not believe it and would make such remarks as: "Impossible! Poetry and medicine do not mix! You're pulling my leg!"

Gossip of course circulated in staid and conservative Rutherford about the handsome and articulate doctor and the possibility of hanky-panky with nurses and patients. Helen Fall reports that "while Dr. Williams may have been the finest baby doctor in Rutherford, her mother-in-law was a little anxious about having this wild Bohemian cross her threshold."[32] But when Dad was sent for to deal with her son's colic, Helen remembers, "I loved him the minute he walked into the house with his sweet smile and gentle voice. I think I recognized right away that I had a buddy—someone who realized that it wasn't easy living at 162 Sylvan Street." After relating many stories of Dad's helpfulness, she mentions her admiration and love of Mom. Once, when the youngest baby, Fred, had a rash, and Dad was not at home, Flossie suggested "an old-fashioned remedy." "Doctor wouldn't care for it," Floss warned, but her prescription of a mixture of "milk of magnesia and witch hazel—half and half" "cleared her it up in a day and a half." Flossie was "a hard woman to get to know," Helen recalls. "She had a veneer of stiffness—possibly primness—but underneath she was the sweetest and nicest person." As for Dad, Mrs. Fall concludes: "He was a dear man."

Louise Wagner

Released from the rein of his professional role, which inhibited any tendency for him to function as a stud, and undoubtedly moderated the advances of his girls at the hospital, he could instead function as a free agent in his social group here in his hometown.

Louise Wagner was an intimate of the folks, a member of Mom's bridge group and the Polytopic Club.[33] Allegedly on one occasion she wanted to comb Dad's hair with a rake. Whether bamboo or steel I don't know, but he apparently escaped when her intention became clear.

Louise was a registered nurse married to a big-voiced, dominating type of male animal who doubtless left much to be desired romantically. Not that Earl wasn't a loving husband and devoted father. On one occasion on a night out at a club in New York City, Louise responded to an urge and taking the baton from the conductor, proceeded to lead the band. And Earl stood by to see that she had her moment in history. But perhaps her champion's type of masculinity left something to be desired, which something could be found in the poet-doctor-friend-husband of her chum Floss.

A 1951 letter to Ezra Pound from my father states, "[a]s far as I know I have never asked a woman for her intimacy."[34] Whether or not this overstates the matter, it is certain that women liked him and pursued him, not a few of them aggressively.

Madeline Spence

Quite a different story was Madeline Spence, née Heyder, native to Newton, New Jersey, and graduate of the Peabody Conservatory of Music in Baltimore. This concert pianist and composer had married a very conscientious bookkeeper who commuted daily to his job with a wood-importing firm on Turtle Cove in the East River. Arriving home evenings he changed his clothes and scurried down to his shop in the cellar, where he lost himself in his craft of woodworking, at which he was indeed of cabinetmaker quality. Weekends he suffered incapacitating migraine headaches when the sublimation of the 9 to 5 job was not available. The *andante senza spirito* of the saw, hammer, and plane emanating from the cellar failed to dampen the *vivace con spirito* of Madeline's Steinway rendering Beethoven's *Appassionata* sonata.[35]

Like so many talented women she had sacrificed a career in the arts she loved for security, I suppose, as a mother and housewife. But there would always remain the lack of fulfillment, the sense of an opportunity aborted, to be replaced by a lackluster life as a piano teacher in a small suburban community in New Jersey. Not that she wasn't appreciated by her peers. She was much in demand for concerts, for the most part local at clubs, churches, etc. At the piano she was a very appealing figure, a slim brunette with bobbed hair naturally waved, a shoulder-strap gown molding generous breasts, and tapering to slim ankles. She was a very attractive woman, vivacious, with a commanding presence at the piano. In no way did her circumstances reduce her awareness of her own ability as an artist. She exuded female magnetism, and in the background, the *andante senza spirito* of the saw, hammer, and plane.

Suddenly, there was Bill Williams. An artist like herself. A poet. A man who had confessed his desire, in a letter to his mother, "to live a passionate life full of striving, full of eager attempts to the whole extent of the power that is in me." And again, "I also wish to do great works of art—to write good poems." These two special people, each a creator, with a gift given to a few and appreciated by even fewer, found each other in the eddy off the main stream of arts, this bedroom of the pawns of Wall Street. There formed a bond, whether spoken or unspoken I don't know, but evidenced in small ways, like the cool, clear, blue October day at the farm in Monroe when the two of them broke away from the group as we crossed the stubble of one of Pa Herman's young apple orchards. Perhaps 50 yards away on an already defoliated tree hung a large, perfect Northern Spy. Laughing and shouting, dodging and jostling, they pulled up to the tree together, only to find the fruit just out of reach. Dad grabbed Madeline around the thighs and held her just high enough to permit picking the apple, then let her slide slowly back to the ground, blushing and breathless. Oh joy! Oh rapture!

On another occasion at Cranberry Lake, while I lay unobserved sunning on top of the "swimming rock" in front of the cottage, the two of them in the water perhaps 12 feet below approached head on doing a slow frog kick and breast stroke, and as they met, Dad's hands enclosed her two breasts. "Oh Bill!" Splutter, blush, and backwater. Small external manifestations of a precious understanding, a melding of values and aspirations, a shared love experience.

Madeline was not in the same league with his previous lady friends and came into his life probably as a patient, but definitely as a member of the local social group to which my parents belonged. Both were married with families, but the vibes from their relationship were sufficiently apparent to her peers to initiate Flossie's comment in a letter dated November 1, 1928: "You are the only attraction in our family for her." Meow! Meow!

Florence Herman Williams

As the packet-boat which is William Carlos Williams trades up and down the Passaic River, it gradually broadens its horizons, venturing down to Newark Bay, past Sandy Hook, and into the ocean swells. There is a gyroscope on his keel, preventing excessive pitch and roll. This is Floss, who will permit the skipper to set any damn course he wishes, but she will always be there to modify his excursions toward reefs and shoal waters. She had come into his life as a teenager, catching him on the bounce when he was rejected by her sister Charlotte. Having established the fact of their engagement, he immediately left for postgraduate medical study at the University of Leipzig. Physically, judging from photos taken at the time, she was a beautiful young woman, with the wasp waist and piled hairdo of the Gibson Girl. At my request her sister Charlotte provided a brief statement of her character as a young woman. From her home in California she wrote: "About Floss, was she a square? I guess compared to me I'd say yes. She was very proper, with a very good mind and a strong will."

So after 15 years of married life, Floss summarized her attitude toward her husband as part of her correspondence from Switzerland in 1927 to 1928. In January 1928, Floss responded to his letter of December 26/27:

> You are an emotional person and so very attractive to women, but we can't have everything and everyone easily. There's always a price to pay, and for myself the price isn't worth the loss of my self-respect or your disappointment and pain. So for me no—if it could be done easily and let go again, there might be moments of impulse that would carry me thru. But it's not for me. Your problem I can't solve for you, but you know that I love you and will never lose faith in you, and knowing that, I leave you free as may be. I'll never judge you harshly. I know too much, compared with what I knew some years ago, and I realize clearly that we don't all work in the same way, and so can't be lumped together for one grand reckoning. I'm by nature reserved—you the opposite. I'm not maternal, tho I love my boys more and more, and I'm not a Lesbian by gosh—I like men—just like them. They never come up

> to my standards of what a man should be. You do—because, I suppose, I know you inside and out, and I love your weakness with your strength.

In Spring 1928 she sent him this letter:

> As I try to sit back and think of you coldly and critically—I say this. I love your moods and your torments. They are part of you, but your emotions do carry you away at times—especially in letters that you write to others (not me) [...]. You and I are two quite different temperaments. I am distant—not easy to make friends with, and not wanting many. You attract everyone—and like people easily. But it's impossible to keep them at arm's length after making advances—unless you burn yourself in devoting yourself to them. You lead a full passionate life—meeting and knowing and loving people, and "getting" them better than most of us can. But you can't give all of yourself and that torments you, because you really don't want to, but you dislike hurting people. Don't let it trouble you too much. I'd rather have you as you are, dear Bunny, than any other way in the world. We are perhaps too different in some things, but I have more tolerance for your temperament than most women could have—and I know that I can let you go if I have to—and will keep on loving you as I do and will welcome you back if you should decide to come back. [...] It is nice to talk to you and try to have you understand that I'm with you heart and soul to the end. It's not possible to say more—but I love to get your letters and they help me to see you and myself clearly. Don't hesitate ever to tell me what you wish.

13

Bringing Up Sonny

The clay of our somatic beings contains genetic factors and thereby presents to our environment a certain indestructible *anlage* which may be manipulated but never destroyed. Without going into blood types and some of the other more sophisticated serological procedures used in the medico-legal determination of parenthood, I offer as incontrovertible evidence of my legitimacy, my mother, Florence Hilda Herman, wife to my father. Should anyone have the temerity to question the source of the seed of my conception then lunar months before my birth, he would thereby demonstrate his ignorance of the character of Flossie, and he would forever after be haunted by tirades of maledictions from her irate ghost. Indeed, Paul and I may safely assume that the dough from which our loaves were formed sprang from the same yeast, the source of which was W.C. Williams, husband to Florence.

There has been much made of child-parent bonding in today's practice of pediatrics, which is not easy to accomplish in the sterile and businesslike atmosphere of the maternity ward. Certainly, there was adequate opportunity for such an experience in my case since I was born at home in the master bedroom, and there is documented evidence in my father's writing that he was present at the time, including a description of my vocal abilities and the adequacy of my genitals.[1] So we can conclude that at least at my launching in the sanctum at 9 Ridge Road we were a closeknit group of three. How much fondling, petting, billing, and cooing and other manifestations of so-called bonding transpired we are not told, but little Oedipus had arrived and initiated the classic triangle. Incidentally, from that moment to the present "the house," as I grew to call it in my childhood, has remained the focus of our comings and goings. Talk about stability, continuity, and security, at least in the physical sense we have had it. Our comedies and tragedies, successes and failures, births and deaths have all occurred in the setting of 9 Ridge Road.

The poem "Promenade" in the little book *Al Que Quiere!* (1917) describes an early morning walk, apparently on the lane below Flossie's uncle's place in Vermont, by toddler son and father, who enjoy pebbles thrown in a rivulet, tiny rafts of fern fragments and twigs floated beneath overhanging foliage, the sudden employment of the magnetism of the cows to draw the child's cold and wet hands (as well probably as his feet) from the brook to the warmth of the barn, and finally to the sunny open field to pick flowers for Mother. Of course, I don't remember, but to read it is to experience a renascence of my father's presence and a reaffirmation of his concern with and interest in the learning process of his son, and to appreciate his ability to guide the child subtly through channels which he himself obviously has already charted and enjoyed—rivulet, rafts, water, cold, cows, warmth, flowers, and back to Flossie. At this tender stage in my earliest formative years, I conclude that I had a gentle and understanding guide to many very basic experiences in settings that not all father-son pairs have the opportunity to share.

PROMENADE

I.

Well, mind, here we have
our little son beside us:
a little diversion before breakfast!

Come, we'll walk down the road
till the bacon will be frying.
We might better be idle?
A poem might come of it?
[...]

III.

[...]
A bunch of little flowers
for Flossie—the little ones
only:
                    a red clover, one
blue heal-all, a sprig of
bone-set, one primrose,

a head of Indian tobacco, this
magenta speck and this
little lavender!
Home now, my mind!—
Sonny's arms are icy, I tell you—
and have breakfast![2]

Other evidence of our father's curiosity and concern about landmarks in the growth and development of both Paul and myself turned up a couple of years ago in the subterranean stacks at the Beinecke Library at Yale. Donald Gallup conducted us down into that air-conditioned catacomb where are preserved the manuscripts and rare editions of many of the modern greats. Pursuing one of Paul Mariani's brainstorms, he and I had gone there to retrieve a folder of Dad's letters to me. Included with the letters there turned up a bonus in the form of childish script and drawings, most dated and identified in Dad's writing. "Billie age 7—Mar. 19–1921 Man coming down to breakfast—Horse in stable—balloon." Believe me, as a sometime father myself, the sketches have nothing of aesthetic appeal which might recommend them for identification and preservation. His was obviously a more catholic eye. I conclude that since he studied and labeled the compositions he must have given them considerable thought and found them significant. It seems we begin to find the minutiae which later will be employed so effectively in the novel *White Mule* (1937) about Flossie's infancy and childhood.

In the Beinecke collection is one of my younger brother Paul's sketches, a crudely framed portrait of the three of us, Dad in the middle, we boys on either side. It interests me because, according to Mom's labels, the most detailed study is of Dad. He is endowed with arms and hands, whiskers, teeth, and a smile. I, on the other hand, am very simplistically reproduced; however, I am drawn with much the longest legs in the group, making me by far the tallest, which after all is only proper for the big brother.

Of course, in these early years Dad was not yet under the kind of pressure from his medical practice that would come later, so there was time to report and observe the actions of his children. However, many events would soon make life complicated, and time would become a more precious commodity. There was a world war, which would cause family tensions. Dad leaning to the English-French allies and Mom sympathizing with the countrymen of her German father. The practice

William Carlos Williams with Paul (center) and William Eric (Sonny) outside his doctor's office, 1919. Courtesy the Poetry Collection of the University Libraries, University at Buffalo, The State University of New York.

was growing rapidly as Dad found acceptance among the other physicians in the community who sent more work his way. A pandemic of influenza would cut down many doctors, thus increasing the burden for the survivors. Dad's Muse, Poetry, would more and more involve him and frustrate him as he became involved not only in the creation, but also in the editing and publication of poems by others. More and more authority, discipline, and character building fell on the shoulders of our mother. Yet she never found it necessary to carry a big stick.

Dad for me would always be in the background, like the lion of the pride, representing ultimate authority, the source of force should its use become necessary, but rarely involved in our daily routine. True the routine of the whole house was modified to accommodate his comings and goings, office hours, etc. But our paths crossed seldom, other than at mealtimes. Before we left for school in the morning, he had departed on his rounds of house calls and hospital visits. He was finishing office hours as we did our homework and were put to bed. Trips for fun and shopping in New York were conducted by Mom, such as a visit to Macy's for camp and school clothes, Christmas shopping in many stores, and treats like Barnum and Bailey's Circus in the spring, and the Hippodrome in the fall. Of course, on major outings like all day at Bronx Park with lunch at the Rocking Stone Restaurant, Dad was the guide. And out-of-state stuff in the car required his presence as driver for the 40 miles to Nanny Herman's farm at Monroe, New York, the 90 miles to Mom's Uncle Einar's farm in Wilmington, Vermont, and the drive to Ocean Avenue in West Haven.

The Monroe trip was often a weekend outing, and we kids learned a lot about our father's character as we joined the stream of traffic going south on Sunday nights out of the Catskills to New York City on that three-lane suicide pike, Route 17. But the Vermont and Connecticut trips were likely to be one-way for Paul and myself. Dad would spend enough time at the shore to dig a peck of clams, and time enough in Wilmington to gather a couple of milk pails of mushrooms, and then scoot back to Rutherford, leaving his mother Nana Williams in charge at the shore, and Mom in command at the farm in Vermont. I know now there was much on his mind as we kids were growing up, most importantly his depression over his failure to gain recognition in his chosen field of poetry, and the frustration he experienced at being an impotent rebel opposing the status quo and questioning the motives of friends in the arts who were fleeing to Europe. Somehow he found the energy to perform both of his roles, physician and poet, quite well, but it meant absenting himself from the family group during much of our leisure and vacation times.

In my case, I found male companionship and models in my peer group in the local community, among camp leaders, and fortunately among several of Dad's fisherman patients, who carted me around to trout streams until I was old enough to drive, at which time I returned the favor. Our father never became the avid fisherman that Paul and I did. Neither had he any interest in hunting. My good friends, the Rybicki brothers initiated me into the gentle art of shooting rats in the local dump with a .22, and hunting blackbirds, ducks, snipe, rabbit, and pheasant with a 12-gauge shotgun in the meadowlands on Rutherford's east border. Renato De Azevedo, the father of another close pal was our brave leader on deep-sea fishing trips out of Sheepshead Bay, and I say "brave" advisedly. To conduct a grubby bunch of eight- to 12-year olds on the train to New York, subway to Sheepshead Bay, all day on the boat untangling lines and baiting hooks, and later steering us back home over the same route, doubtless reeking of dead clams and fish fillets, each kid hugging his own gunnysack of the day's loot, was heroic, and we loved him. He later owned a Reo Flying Cloud that was the first car in my experience to climb the hill south of Denville on the old Route 46 in high gear. It was a route I took often as he very generously took the same grubby bunch for weekends in a log cabin he owned at Indian Lake.

And finally, there was my very favorite man, Pa Herman, he of the handsome moustache that was tucked under the lower lip with the right hand before drying on his napkin. He of the aroma of carnation cologne and White Owl cigars, the gentleman farmer who did his daily "constitutional" down the country road and through the farm buildings with his faithful canine entourage—Mike, Tip, and Tootsie, always a pair of clippers in his pocket, clipping, shaping, and trimming his beloved grape vines, roses, nut and fruit trees, and a gorgeous avenue of double French lilacs. Evenings we played Chicago in the billiards room in the basement adjoining the wine cellar.[3] Nights we slept on the sleeping porch on the east end of the house, facing Harriman House across the valley on its mountaintop. My grandmother Nanny tucked us in, gave us a smooch, and took off to turn out the cats and dogs and otherwise secure the house for the night. He was a Giants fan and often needled me in his guttural "Cherman" accent full of "mitt," "yah," and "von," about the Yankees and Babe Ruth, before we drifted off to sleep. A quiet-spoken, gentle man with a sly wit suited to the likes of us kids, he nonetheless had his code, and commuted every day from Harriman to the city. One of the few material souvenirs I have of my grandfather Paul Herman is one of his business cards, on the back of which in his beautiful script appears this sentence: "Work is not man's punishment; it is *his reward* and *his strength, his glory* and *his pleasure.* P.H."

How can a mere father compete with heroes of this caliber? Dad was a busy man, preoccupied with medical problems and poetry. I'm sure he was aware of a young adolescent's need for a male figure to pattern himself after, and I'm sure he was torn by his inability to find more time for us kids. Certainly, his interest and authority are evidenced by the fact of my owning firearms—he must have given permission. On my reaching age 17, a brand-new 1931 Ford Roadster appeared in our garage. We have photographic evidence that Dad in his knickerbockers and carrying a walking stick climbed Mt. Chase with Paul and me up in Aroostook County, Maine, around 1923, and a year or two later the three of us spent an evening at Savin Rock, a Connecticut version of Coney Island, testing the games of skill and chance and having a group portrait made as we posed before the corny commercial backdrop.

But all these images are mere incidents in my childhood and pubertal stages, highlights of turbulent years in the life of an introspective kid who annually was shunted off to camp as soon as school closed and was left with relative strangers for a year while the folks explored bohemia abroad. Finally, my brother and I were shipped off to a Swiss school for 12 months, that package including Mom's absence from the parental nest in Rutherford and her presence in Europe as an agent of authority and TLC.

William Eric with William Carlos Williams at Coppet College, Switzerland, 1927. Courtesy the Poetry Collection of the University Libraries, University at Buffalo, The State University of New York.

I have never been certain how my father influenced my attitude toward the fair sex, whether by precept or by example. Certainly, there was no preaching and no commandments were laid down to define the behavior I would adhere to. Suffice it to say there was an aura of morality at home that didn't have to be spoken. Nevertheless, this in no way curbed or distorted the normal curiosity and exploration that comes with early manhood. Until my father became a famous man and his life came into the public domain, I had always assumed his was a very proper and moral sex life, and I patterned myself after him. What the historians may uncover or conclude about him is water under the bridge as far as I'm concerned, and water that had no influence on me.

I would guess Paul and I and the neighborhood gang had as good a basic training in the anatomy of female and male reproductive organs as any bunch of kids for miles around. After all, Dad's office was attached to the house, and *Gray's Anatomy* and *Williams Obstetrics* were right inside the office door on the shelf to the left. Not available for such public display were Frank Harris's stories of his sexual prowess, and the tales of Boccaccio, which got well-thumbed over the years.[4]

But I think in the final analysis my peer group did most to alert and educate me. Our home was and is on the border between the commercial and residential parts of Rutherford, so that we had a mix among our pals of "rough guys" and "nice kids." The "toughs" were for the most part children of immigrants who had a very practical knowledge of how all these sex parts went together, possessed a working vocabulary descriptive of the anatomy and physiology of the parts, and were most overt in their attempts at consummation of their desires. North of our property line there was a definite awareness, and looking back over the years, I realize that one of our friends wasn't called "Pussy" because he was overly fond of the blossoms on willow trees in the spring. South of the line, on the other hand, we "nice" kids were molded in the Victorian traditions, and although our juices flowed just as hot, sublimation was the rule of the day. In fact, I recall a letter from my father in reply, when as an underclassman I had written extolling Wordsworth's lines:

> One impulse from a vernal wood
> May teach you more of a man
> Of moral evil and of good,
> Than all the sages can.[5]

His answer was to the effect that at the same age he too had been a subscriber, but that it would be well to wait before adopting this philosophy as a way of life. For the immediate future abstinence was to be commended, with a prize at the end of the trail consisting of that special part of femininity chosen to share one's connubial bliss. In other words, young feller, keep your pecker in your pants.

Atypical as was our family life in my teen years, somehow we all came through as a family unit. The Great Depression was ending, I was off to Williams College in Massachusetts and Paul was prepping at Mercersburg in Pennsylvania. An era of artistic acceptance and gratification began in 1936 with the appearance of James Laughlin IV, founder of New Directions.[6] We boys had become more rational creatures capable of some degree of self-navigation and self-discipline. Family outings became more formal—dinner at a favorite restaurant, the Mont d'Or in the East Fifties perhaps, followed by a play.

We were at times included in invitations to social functions of our elders, and our goings and comings early and late no longer cost Dad any loss of sleep. The bickerings and battles of sibling rivalry were history—each of us went his own way. In fact we came to respect each other, becoming tolerant of each other's idiosyncrasies, at times serving as confidants for each other, and to this day we maintain an intimate neutrality which can flame into violent partisanship given the proper provocation. The necessity for parental police action was over, ending one source of tissue wear and tear for the folks. But still looming on the horizon as we finished our academic years were three major parental concerns: (1) how we would earn our bread, (2) with whom we would mate to propagate another generation, and (3) how we would weather World War II.

In my case the blinders with which I'd been saddled by the community all my life were snugged down lest I deviate from fate's decree that I become a physician. Off to the sides on occasion were visions of a life as a writer, or especially a career in forestry, but like a well-trained little horsey, I would stick close to the rail and gallop all the way to the finish line. Not that I was coerced. The subject of medicine as a career as far as Dad was concerned was always open for discussion, and, as I have reported elsewhere, the profession was never the greatest of his loves.[7] It served him so he could write poetry. It was presented to me as a damn good way to make a living; one wasn't often hungry as a doctor. And there was always reinforcement from friends, neighbors, and countrymen: "Your father will be so proud" or "a chip off the old block" or "You'll be a good doctor, I know."

The end for the folks was in sight, at least as far as I was concerned.

Brother Paul was an entirely different *espèce d'animal,* capable of rebellion and making his own thoughts known, let the chips fall where they may. We were fulfilling the augury of Pa Herman, who years before had branded us: I was "the professor," and Paul was "the capitalist."

When the Japanese accomplished their "surprise" attack on Pearl Harbor on that Sunday that "would live in infamy," to quote our great leader, I was 27 years old, and still an apprentice in the gentle art of patching heads and healing fevered bodies.[8] I was a very naïve young man, versed in the sciences of the birds, bees, and assorted advanced animals of the order mammalia. But my exposure to what the kids now call "Social Studies" (with a grimace, I might add—like a dose of castor oil) had been minimal. Political science, history, economics, and psychology were insignificant impedimenta in the curriculum of a pre-medical student. However, I was well aware that FDR's ascension to the throne in Washington, D.C., was akin, in my father's opinion, to the second coming of Christ, and by interference his was "the kingdom and the power and the glory."[9]

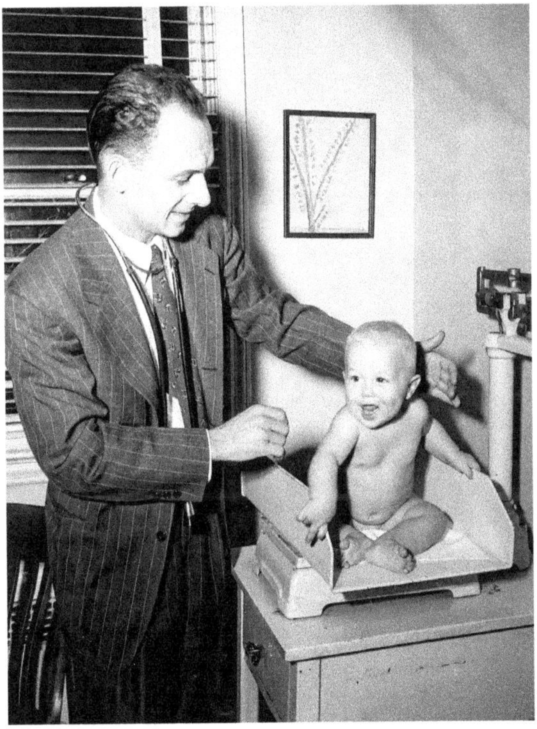

Dr. William Eric Williams, 1950, weighing a baby in the doctor's office at 9 Ridge Road. Courtesy the Poetry Collection of the University Libraries, University at Buffalo, The State University of New York.

I enjoyed a great unawareness of power politics and arms cartels, and share the profound naivete and gullability of we who comprise the electorate. On the other hand, I was aware of a streak in my father's personality that had been alluded to in family verbal intercourse and was apparently never satisfied. That was a wish to do something of importance on a larger scale, like go to the South Pole as the physician with the Scott expedition, or go to France with the American Expeditionary Force in The Great War. I suspect both his hero worship of Roosevelt and his unsatisfied desire to do a great service for mankind were uppermost in his mind as I toured around on ambulance duty that fateful Sunday night, listening to the tales coming over the airways and absorbing the indignation and anti–Japanese sentiment of the man in the street. And I believe my presence at Third Naval District headquarters the next morning was a subconscious desire to please my father. Suffice it to say I was there, at 90 Church Street, in a mob that looked like a sale in Macy's basement. When I had been identified by a Marine guard as a physician interested in making the navy my career for the duration (I was recognizable by the medical whites which were, and are, uniform of the day for physicians on ambulance duty), all red tape was dispensed with, an elevator took me up to where they make officers, and approximately one coffee break later I was in the navy. That evening at home the atmosphere was quite subdued. No strong emotion either pro or con, no criticism of my impetuous volunteering, but an air of inevitability and let's get the job done. In a few months

William Eric Williams, U.S. Naval Reserve, 1941. Courtesy the Poetry Collection of the University Libraries, University at Buffalo, The State University of New York.

I was in a thatch-roofed post office in Vaitape, Bora Bora, en route to islands further west with the first wave of Sea Bees.

My interest in philately would be fed by many such places in the next couple of years. I was on my own. The war had precipitated what was really my first adult decision that was entirely of my own making. My father and I had become equals, and we would correspond regularly for the next four years, sharing medical experience and anecdotes, and reporting what we knew of the progress of the war, so far as the censor would allow.[10] I'm sure writing to me and Paul regularly on a weekly basis for the time we were overseas was at times a backbreaking burden, but somehow he made it to the end of the war—just!

14

The Doctor

Each physician is endowed with their own mystique.[1] I guess you could call it their bedside manner. But it is more than that really. The image of the physician is a conglomeration in the public's eye of someone who has been exposed to the longest and most difficult educational process of all the professions. They bring to the ailing patient a profound knowledge not only of anatomy and physiology, but an understanding of the workings of the mind as well. They have been tested by fire in the mill of the hospital and clinic during their internship, and, at least in Dad's case, with damn little renumeration except a place to sleep and three sometimes not so "squares." Death, pain, disease, deformity, and the demented are the physician's daily fare, to which they become inured. The physician is a sage. A priest. They are often the first to be called in all variety of emergencies, many of which can scarcely be called medical. The physician is patient, not only in hearing your story, but in waiting for the *quid pro quo* as well. And most of all, they are available, as near to you as your telephone.

And this image is not lost on the physicians themselves. The doctor's ego is a well-recognized entity and is nourished by their patients. And though Dad enjoyed his status as physician, and at times in things medical proved a martinet, this was tempered with humility and humanity. An iconoclast, yes. A hypocrite no.

Dad was well trained and absorbed that to which he had been exposed. He came from the University of Pennsylvania Medical School to Rutherford via residencies in New York City and postgraduate work in Leipzig. He had traveled abroad meaningfully and had hobnobbed with intellectuals at home and at college. He could communicate in five languages. At least one prominent New York specialist had offered him a place in his practice.

So, his first dispensary in 1910 was his parents' former pantry, his mode of transportation a bicycle, and his first patient a shy young thing with ringworm of the scalp.[2] His professional training having been intimately associated with a series of hospitals, he sought appointment to the staff of one of the local institutions. First, he was turned down cold by the Hackensack Hospital. They didn't want anyone from the southern part of Bergen Country. Since he was interested in, and specifically trained for, the care of children, he offered to give his services without renumeration to the county orphanage at Hackensack. This he was granted. But only for a period of two years. He was so successful and had apparently brought the job such an aura of glamour that it was taken from him, converted into a salaried position, and dispensed to another local doctor. It was in Passaic that the poor dog was finally thrown a bone. He was given a position as a courtesy staff member, in which status he served for 20 years, before being appointed to the regular staff.

Meanwhile he continued to keep abreast of the medical times by attending weekly clinics in Pediatrics at Post Graduate Hospital and Babies' Hospital in New York City. The Passaic Hospital was a closed book to him as far as Pediatrics was concerned because of a one-man band man named Van Riper who had a stranglehold on the service and wasn't about to release it. In obstetrics his abilities were more appreciated, particularly by the nurses, who didn't hesitate to call him when there was a difficult delivery and someone needed help.

In his hometown most families were already committed to other physicians. He took the job of school doctor, and on one occasion, having sent a child home with the diagnosis of scarlet fever, was branded an impudent young whippersnapper by the adult's family doctor, and the diagnosis denied. Fortunately, a third physician was consulted and Dad vindicated. He became physician to the town's baby clinic, held in the old city hall in a room across from police headquarters. He was physician to the town's not inconsiderable black population because no one else would take care of them. And according to Mother, they were damn good patients, followed instructions to the letter, and they *Paid Cash.* Gradually, at least in Rutherford, there was recognition by his fellow doctors.

On the morning of September 10, 1914, a week before his thirty-first birthday, I imagine my Dad descending the back stairs of 9 Ridge Road and striding across the yard to the garage, his suit coat agape, his black bag in the left hand, car keys in the right, and between his teeth a gaggle of letters to be dropped at the post office.[3] In the left upper pocket of his vest is a red leatherette notebook, measuring 14 × 7 cm, containing about 70 pages, and on the first page his handwritten report of his work for the week as the Rutherford Medical Inspector of Schools. And so, a record of my father's work at Rutherford, New Jersey, public schools began. This is obviously the notebook of a conscientious school physician, and for the first pages all entries concern school matters: mumps, impetigo, too many children in the kindergarten room, nits, measles, names of officials and teachers to telephone or meet with. Suddenly on page four: "what is it that is so excellent in the Japanese artist but that they have seen their fish their fowls their horses in intimate completeness." Such interjections irrelevant to school business at the beginning of the little red notebook are crossed out with a big X, but still readable. At the end, he reversed the pages and used them exclusively for images, sketches, and quotations from the speech of patients, with no big X's.[4]

On page 64 (reversed) in neat, intensive handwriting, he exclaims:

> I bless the muscles of their thighs, their needs that are limber, their hair that is like new grass, their eyes that are not always dancing, their postures so naïve and graceful, their voices that are full of fright and other passions, their transparent shams and their mimicry of adults—the softness of their bodies—

The little red notebook exhibits the details of the nitpicking daily drudgery of the school doctor that helped him make his report to the Board of Health. But it is also caught and held like a Brueghel canvas to the human parade, the chips and flakes that fly about for the sensitive mind to appreciate and harvest. Here is a handwritten record of the workings of the mind of a poet-physician on his daily rounds, including, on page 63 (reversed), a prescription for life support for himself, hurriedly scribbled: "If I did not have verse I would have died or been a thief."

In his second summer of practice, he was asked to cover another doctor who was on vacation. For this responsibility it was necessary to have a horse-drawn rig sent up to 131 West Passaic Avenue every morning. The livery stable on Erie Avenue obliged. Sometime later, the ear of the son of a prominent local family having failed to respond to homeopathic blandishments, Dad was consulted and steered the acute mastoid into proper therapeutic channels. On another occasions, Dr. Armstrong, who earlier had dubbed Dad "whippersnapper," turned over to him the home delivery of a well-to-do lady of the community. The young associate of still another physician urgently called Dad to a home in Lyndhurst, where he found fetal distress due to transverse arrest, and doctor-in-distress due to an enraged and threatening father. With the other man administering the ether, he was able to do a quick version and extraction of a living baby. He personally recounted to me years later the tale of a woman residing scarcely a block from his office. It was an apartment over a shop facing on Park Avenue. The patient was at term and critically ill, with a septic fever. Labor had started. A sanguine-purulent discharge issued from the birth canal. As in most obstetrical emergencies the old maxim was to empty the uterus of its content. With the patient in extremis, he slipped on a shoulder-length glove, manually dilated the cervix, and ruptured the membranes. There was a gush of pus and macerated fetus all over him, the bed, and the floor. But miraculously the patient survived. Her convalescence naturally was stormy. For months, foci of infection cropped out in her skin, urinary tract, and skeleton. But from this too she recovered. "A tough baby," was his final summation.

Possibly one of the happiest happenings in this whole medical career was the referral to Dad of the population of Guinea Hill in Lyndhurst. This nidus of Latins in what was otherwise a nondescript polyglot community had been the patients of a now aging Dr. Calhoun. It was love at first sight. The Monacos, Gentiles, Caggianos, Sinopolises, etc., etc., etc., took him to their ample bosoms. It was home away from home. He delivered their babies, cured their sicknesses, and relieved the suffering of the incurable. Not many of them had phones, but when he was summoned to care for one, he could count on a full morning of house-to-house visits. The word was passed. The doctor is here. All the saved-up ailments were unloaded. Payment was a glass of wine here, a loaf of bread there, a bag of ripe figs from the tree out back, a kitten, a promise (fulfilled) to come in the fall and make a barrel of wine, a hug and kiss, as well as a few dollars. These patients were simple, sincere, hard-working peasants, with their community oven fired up in the morning for all to bake their bread, tucked away on their goat-infested, sun-ridden knoll back of the cemetery.

"Hey Doc. How many kids you got?"
"Two little boys," answers Dad.
"Whatsa da matta Doc, you sleep?"

Chorus of eavesdroppers up and down the street. "Cackle, cackle, cackle," and nodding of bandanaed heads in windows, doorways, and at the clothesline. Later at the office a postpartum visit from mother and child, Dad amazed to see the infant's eyes shining, disease-free. Boric acid solution and argyrol, the accepted therapy of the day having failed to heal the infant's conjunctivitis, the grandmother had taken over. While milking the nannie out back she had caught a cup of goat urine. Faithfully dropping this into the bambino's eyes over a period of days, she had cured them. *Touché, dottore*! A primitive primer in chemotherapy.

Office hours, the heart of a doctor's practice, one to three in the afternoon, seven until God knows when in the evening—the domestic cycle of our home was arranged to accommodate them. Meals were on time, and so were we. Appetite sated, and his napkin rolled and tucked into its ring, Dad would disappear through the swinging door to the kitchen, cross the small back hall, and descend two steps to his office on the north side of the house. Through 50 years of active practice, this was his solo arena. Never did he feel the need for a receptionist or nurse. No buffer to modify in any way the doctor-patient relationship. A small lab and toilet abutted the house wall. Out front the waiting room, the walls grass-papered, simply furnished, separated by a narrow dressing and storage space from the examining room in the rear. Dominating the examining room against the east wall was the big desk with the hinged top that concealed the typewriter. A small residual of floor space in the middle of the room was encircled by a chair, a glass-enclosed instrument case, a couch, a baby scale, and an examining table. It was comfortable, intimate, and informal, an atmosphere conducive to confidence and the unburdening of secret problems.

His was a general practice with sub-specialties in Obstetrics and Pediatrics. Afternoons were largely well babies and antepartum visits. On one hot afternoon as I was cutting the side lawn under the office windows, it struck me that this was a helluva way to make a living. There was no air conditioning. Babies were screaming before, during, and after their examinations. There was a stream of patients extending out the waiting room door, down the office steps, along the walk, and down the second set of stone steps to the sidewalk. Carriages were parked all over the front lawn so I couldn't possibly cut it. There were a couple of stationary fans that blew the air around a bit in the waiting and examining rooms, and of course all the doors and windows were open. But it must have been stifling to work in that environment. Somehow they were all seen. For each a note was made on his card in the file in the upper right-hand drawer. "Big. Gained 20 oz. Anemic." "Beautiful. Vigorous. Vaccinated." "Lice, Rickets. CLO. Tinct. Larkspur." All positive. No negatives. Meat only, with the scrap cut away, but a note of some kind on every visit. Detailed instructions on feeding the well baby and treating those who were ill, to be rigidly followed unless you were looking for a new doctor. The willful child obstinately refusing to cooperate summarily dismissed with the admonition to the parents to instill discipline or not return. The last one out the door finally. Ten or a dozen urines waiting in the lab. The stench of boiling urea, Fehling solution, and acetic acid permeating the room. A few blood specimens in their cylindrical cardboard containers to be mailed to Trenton. Finally, the session at Mom's desk in the living room, emptying out his wallet (the folding type, carried in the right hip pocket) and dictating, over Mother's shoulder, names, credits and debits, which she entered in the black leather-covered call book. She in turn had her own card file, and at the end of each month did the billing—by hand.

House calls were his particular *pièces de résistance.* They meant people. People at home were in their natural settings, with all the interactions of personalities and environment. "How can you know a patient until you see him in his home?" Here was grist for the mill. Here the dog and his nose could explore and sample until sated, like the bee burdened with pollen struggling home to the hive. The orgasm of unloading, food for the soul, satiety in prose and verse. "Put it down while it's hot." He would come in at night and go right to the typewriter. It was our lullaby at home. We went to sleep with it and woke to its tatata ta tata in the morning, always the irregular rhythm of the two-finger typist.

The fee received was really of no particular concern to him. Unless called as a consultant, he never charged for neo-natal well baby care in the hospital. If Mom had not been a damn practical manager he'd have been lost. "How much money do you have in your wallet, Bill?" "Gee, I don't know, Floss." "Did the Smiths pay you?" "I don't remember, but I'll ask them the next time they come in." He identified with the total situation on his calls in his patients' homes, and this was his compensation. It could drive Mom to the wall with frustration.

But all the calls weren't aesthetic experiences. In the early 1900s people were dying of things like typhoid and diphtheria and whooping cough. Malaria was still endemic here in New Jersey. Salvarsan was available for syphilis, but the treatment of tuberculosis was still primitive. TB sanatoriums were jammed. Dad was a member of the Bergen County Mosquito Commission and carried a badge with his name engraved on the obverse to prove it.[5] He went on inspection trips of the meadows along the Hackensack River to observe the progress of the ditching that would doom the breeding ground of the anopheles. We kids were sometimes invited, donning hip boots and slogging along behind on junkets out to the cedar swamps or along Berry's Creek and its tributaries, the areas now occupied by those two eyesores, the Meadowlands Race Track and Giants Stadium.

The year that damn near did him in was 1918. The great influenza pandemic put a crushing load on every practicing physician, many of whom died, increasing the burden on the survivors. There was a critical shortage of manpower in other areas as well. And not enough grave diggers to get the dead underground. The bodies piled up. In more rural communities they were stored in cold outbuildings to stay frozen until the spring thaw. Dad's office was closed. That time he really got a bellyful of his beloved house calls. There were days when there was no sleep. Home to shave and eat, change the shirt, and out again. The friend visited at 8 a.m. was dead at 4 p.m. Sixty or more calls in 24 hours, dreading but searching for the first signs of pneumonia, the killer. The prescription—sponging, whiskey, and aspirin. Mom was stricken with the disease and taken to Florida by her mother to convalesce. My brother Paul and I had it but without complication.

With spring, surcease of the pandemic, but that fall appeared another specter of the times, polio. Dad instructed I was to be left at the farm in Monroe, New York, where I had summered, until such time as he sounded the all-clear. Until the advent of the Salk vaccine in the 1950s, every child with fever and headache in summertime was presumed to have polio, at least by parents. There was then and there is now no treatment for the disease once contracted. The prospect of a crippled child on crutches, or worse, made the families, understandably, panic.

It was a disease that put the doctor-patient relationship under severe strain. Being a children's doctor, Dad saw a lot of it. Some years there was much crippling and many deaths. Other years it was relatively mild, like the year the seven, or was it eight, Franklin boys had it and all without residual. It was an age dominated by diagnosis, the Osler heritage.[6] Therapeutics as we know it today was unknown.

Dad lived to see and use the "miracle drugs." It is a term glibly parroted by writers and the general public. To the old-timers in the medical profession in the 1930s and 1940s the effect of these medicines was truly unbelievable. Miracle—"an effect in the physical world which surpasses all known human or natural powers." It literally changed a way of life. Pneumonia became a $10 instead of a $100 disease. Mastoid surgery became a rarity. Some old-timers never really got the message. I spoke with well-educated and respected members of the medical community in the 1950s who, 20 years after the introduction of the sulfa drugs, and 15 years after penicillin came into common use, maintained that the cure brought about had nothing to do with drugs, but were due to germ mutations which had resulted in less malignant and therefore less invasive bacteria. Dad was not one of these. He was too close to the firing line to be influenced by anything the brass in the specialties could say, secure in their ivory towers, technicians dependent upon the doctors like himself for referral, and thereby sustenance. We all misused the drugs, Dad included. His tendency for an acute bacterial infection was to give a large intramuscular dose of penicillin "to kill most of the germs," and then let the natural resistance of the patient take care of the balance. Sometimes it apparently worked. Sometimes he was forced into using more drug when the patient relapsed. What he was doing was killing off the susceptible bacteria and leaving the resistant strains to grow and thrive and return to haunt him. The same error is still being made. Dad got the message early and corrected his ways.

Very early in the era of sulfa drugs, in fact only weeks after the headlines from Boston about the Roosevelt throat infection,[7] a sick young man with an obvious strep lymphangitis of an extremity appeared in his office one evening. Dad had a few grains of sulfadiazine in the office. The patient was the son of another physician, on his way home for Christmas, and just stopping off to see his girl. He was not planning to stay over but was going home that night. Dad gave him the first dose in the office, outlined the regime to be followed, and told him to get the hell home to his father as fast as he could. The young man did just that. Dad had a very gratifying call the next day from the physician-father, who also had been enlightened on the sulfa drugs and appreciated how grave the situation could have become without prompt therapy. I see the patient (a not-so-young man now) on occasion, and he still speaks of Dad as the guy who saved his life.

It was during the years of World War II that Dad defined for me in one of his letters his philosophy and goals in medicine. First, to be available. Medicine is a full-time commitment. The physician's responsibility is first to his patient, taking precedence over all others, including family. Second, every physician has his limitations, none is a god. He would therefore diagnose and treat to the limit of his capabilities, then seek consultation if dissatisfied with the progress of the case. "Be objective in your evaluation, avoid the subjective, and never hesitate to admit your ignorance or inability to diagnose or treat." And finally, the remuneration is of secondary importance. All of which would be considered heretical in today's medical community.

To him medicine was a priesthood. His availability was legend. At mealtimes the phone was brought to his elbow on an extension cord, and I vividly recall my corn flakes, tuna salad, and roast beef sliding down my throat to an accompaniment of grains of aspirin, tablespoon of dextri-maltose, teaspoons of syrup of ipecac, and drops of ephedrine in oil dictated to sufferers at the other end of the line. At night, calls were taken on a wall phone in the upstairs hall, not at the bedside, lest he fall back to sleep instead of slipping into his trousers over the pajama pants en route to the delivery room. Even in his private sanctum in the attic, during all the years he used that space as his study, an extension of the phone was run up to his desk.

As to the physician's limitations, I think he was his own severest critic, and not always with justification. Here was a man making his living in an inexact science cited to diagnose and allegedly cure the ills of mankind. In reality there was little the physician could do in the way of "healing," other than the instances in which a surgeon could whack out a chunk of diseased tissue, hoping the while that he had completely circumvented the afflicted part. True one could dose with iron for anemia, with arsenicals and mercury for syphilis, quinine for malaria, and salicylates for the rheumatoid. Barbiturates and narcotics were held in reserve to provide the patient a veneer of well-being while the body's natural defenses proceeded with the healing process. But to a man whose heart and soul were concerned with creation, specifically poems; whose genius lay in his ability to find, mold, and polish the materials of his art; who in his avocation knew no limitations, held to no authority, and was his own djinni; to this man how imperfect must have been the other phase of his life, and how frustrating the dictates of this other discipline, the practice of medicine. I'm sure he felt restricted and dissatisfied in dealing with many illnesses. He had a few respected consultants in various fields whom he would turn to, whose brains he would pick until every stone was turned. But his honesty and idealism would never find the satisfaction in medicine that would come from his writing.

And finally, remuneration for services. This was an uncomfortable subject for Dad that he never really solved. He never, like most physicians, put a price on his time, charging so much on an hourly basis. This community is brimming with the tales of his former patients who were seen for various complaints, and who were never asked to pay a fee. I know he worked on a sliding scale, and I know he was aware of the domestic background of all those who consulted him. I'm sure his conscience wouldn't allow him to charge a fee, no matter what his service had been, that would cause the patient the least hardship. And he never sent a dunning letter.[8]

15

Money

Like every other individual born and living in an industrial nation, Dad of necessity had to live with money.[1] As a basic premise, let's say its presence was resented. The money market sickened him. Wall Street, Madison Avenue, Big Business, all these American symbols and idols were of another world. The fact that people would make money, just to be able to make more money, more than any man and his family could ever use in a lifetime, by joining the money lenders, was not only contrary to the Christian ethic, but completely against the grain of William Carlos Williams. There was something about fee for service that detracted from the intent and quality of the service. It was difficult for him to be businesslike. To keep a ledger and send out bills seemed to inject a Scrooge-like quality into the doctor-patient relationship. He was famous for his warm flow of human kindness in his bedside manner. He was the artificial kidney that filtered the patient's vital juices and restored them purified. The gratitude in the patient's heart, and the restored health in their eye was compensation enough. How does one come away from the relationship like this with one party a debtor? Why demean the symmetry and harmony of the exchange with a fee?

Money. He lived with it and by it because he had to. Fortunately, he had Mom, who knew the value of a dollar and was instrumental in keeping the accounts straight and the green flowing in. But his indifference to his bank balance, casualness in giving, and charity in adjusting medical fees was often maddening for her. I remember a half dollar Dad gave me one day at lunch time to bank at school. I must have been eight or nine years old at the time, and Mom was out of the room when he gave it to me. The glitter and mass of the thing really shook me. I had retired under the dining room table with it, never having been entrusted with such a sum of money before. The sun at noon strikes this floor area, and the glitter of the light reflected from the mint coin was to my childish mind like the lifting of the lid from a pirate hoard. On returning from the kitchen and resuming her seat, Mom's eye caught the coin, and there ensued a fair to middling verbal donnybrook, with Mom emerging the winner. I didn't bank the four-bit piece. Back it went into the folding, stamped leather change purse that Dad always had in his side trousers pocket. As I recall there was substituted a pair of Buffalo nickels.[2]

Dad's income was always modest. If he netted $15,000, it was a big year. The family had a few conservative stocks, a savings account, and a minimum of life insurance. Mom inherited some stocks from her father, and that was the extent of their investments. Some time after World War II, an acquaintance who was retired from the business world volunteered to advise them on a contemplated investment of a modest sum. With the three of them seated in the living room, their adviser asked for a review of their "portfolio." Dad hadn't been enchanted by the prospect of the meeting in the first place, but this term simply turned him off. The pomposity of the man's language and demeanor infuriated him. He was on his feet and somehow found an excuse to leave the room. No portfolio-man he. Mom concluded the meeting as politely as she could, and, as I recall, purchased some shares in a mutual fund.

He read with complete sympathy Thorstein Veblen's theory of "Conspicuous Consumption."[3] He thought "two cars in every garage" the verbiage of a mind sold out to "the money boys." He tremendously enjoyed Dr. B's story, told in the dressing room at Passaic General Hospital, concerning the medical hack made wealthy by resetting normal gall bladders at several hundred a throw. An honest anesthesiologist having become disenchanted with being accomplice to the endless chain of normal bellies finally had his fill. Confronting the hacker in the dressing room one morning, he quasi-seriously proposed that he keep a loaded .45 in his top desk drawer, and every time he had a new sucker lined up for the cholecystectomy, the .45 should be held against the prospect's full skull, and the patient should be told that for 300 dollars he (the hacker) would not take out his gall bladder. Ostentation, greed, chicanery hiding behind false fronts. The end justifying the means. There were a lot of people in Dad's rogues' gallery, Richard M. Nixon high among them.

An enigma that has long fascinated but baffled me is a graph of the New York stock market averages from January 1928 to September 1932.

It is pasted to the wall in the attic back of his old desk—the dizzy climb in 1928 and 1929, the precipitous fall in September to October 1929, and it stops abruptly with the gradual upturn in September 1932. Why is it there? Was he placing a hex on Wall Street? Did it make him happy to see the curve go ever downward? Or was it all placed there in retrospect in later years to record a great emotional crisis? Could it have been a tribute to one of his heroes, FDR, who stepped in with a firm hand at that time? Suffice it to say it was in a conspicuous place in his *sanctum sanctorum* in such a way that he must have seen it every time he approached his desk. Not that it is enshrined. The accompanying pieces on the wall include a child's crayon drawing and a menu from a seafood restaurant. If his object had been to anathematize the marketplace, why does it keep such innocent and prosaic company?

But lest we be left with a distorted image of an altruistic masochist laying down with his life for his parishioners, stealing just enough time between cases to nourish the pulse of life in his artistic world, attend and digest this passage from a letter to Ezra Pound, revealing another facet of this complex man:

Nov. 6, 1928

Dear Ezrie:

Nothing will ever be said of better understanding regarding my work than your article in The Dial. I must thank you for your great interest and discriminating defense of my position. Without question you have hit most of the trends that I am following with the effect that you have clarified my designs on the future which in turn will act as encouragement and strength for me.

Naturally I consider myself a fool for not getting out of Medicine. I do not consider myself a fool for having been a physician for the past twenty years. That was accurately figured out in its relations to my disposition and mental capabilities. It has all turned out precisely as I foresaw, save only that at my present age I planned to withdraw from active competition with the world and close up the gaps in my expositions, continuing at this till I was shovelled under or went daffy or satisfactorily convinced myself that I had failed.

I am now engaged in cutting out much of my medical work under the guise of becoming a "specialist." Within a few months I will have done with evening office hours, that hellish drag. But it is not going fast enough. I can't quit cold for I would only torment myself into the grave if I did so. I ain't built that way, I mean to withstand financial worries or to discover ways of living aside from the work of my hands. I simply can't.[4]

Twenty-five years later he had still been unable to "quit cold." He had still been unable to withstand financial worries without the work of his hands. Health was failing. Memory was failing. The opportunity "to withdraw from active competition with the world" had never been seized, and never would be in this world.

16

Flossie

Florence Hilda Herman was born in New York City, April 18, 1890, of immigrant parents, her mother Nanny Hafslund, pure Norwegian and very proud of it, and her father Paul Herman, native of Breslau in Germany. She was the second daughter, and a great disappointment to her mother and older sister, both of whom had wanted a male child. Even her father's first expression on being told was "[t]hat's too bad." And the midwife herself observed, "[y]ou poor little mite, about five pounds I guess." And further, "[y]ou're a homely little runt."[1]

She was small and sucked poorly, much to her mother's disgust. Within the first week she lost almost a pound in weight and developed a green diarrhea. She tossed and screamed. A physician was finally summoned at her father's insistence, much now to the midwife's disgust, feeling loss of authority and displacement. He found a temperature of 105°F, and checking her weight confirmed a loss of at least a pound. "The child's sick—very sick," was his diagnosis, "feed her barley water for three days." She refused feedings for the most part, vomiting what little they could get down. Several days later, the apartment in the interval having become bedlam due to the infant's incessant crying and failure to eat, her father brought home a can of condensed milk, added a tablespoonful to some water in a bottle, and miraculously the infant ate it, not one but two bottlesful. Fortunately, an abscessed ear had ruptured, leaving a yellow stain on the bedspread. From then on the infant ate and grew, but the final trauma to her developing psyche was the return home of her older sister Charlotte, now five years old, who had been boarded out during the *accouchement*. Demanding to see her new baby brother, and being told it was a girl, like herself, she took one look and slapping the baby's face as hard as she could, remarked, "[t]he nasty thing." Before she was eight months old the baby had whooping cough, brought to her by her sister, further handicapping her growth and development, but she survived the first winter. The following year, about the time of her first birthday, she was examined by a physician who threw a fright into her mother. She was barely 17 pounds in weight, and walked feebly. Her muscle tone was poor, her appetite zilch, her color pale. The doctor prognosticated she would not survive the summer if she wasn't taken from the city—at once! The specter of tuberculosis following pertussis in a child was very real at that time. The doctor had said he didn't like the baby's chest, "her lungs, you understand." His prescription was to take her to the country and feed her good food.

So it was determined, after a family conference, including Flossie's Auntie Olga, that mother and two daughters would go to Wilmington, Vermont, escorted as far as Troy on the Hudson Night Boat by the auntie, thence by train to Hoosick Falls, then by narrow-gauge railway, the so-called Hoot, Toot and Whistle, following the course of the Deerfield River, to Wilmington. Finally, three or four miles by horse and wagon to an isolated farm about a mile south of the Molly Stark Trail. In residence were an elderly Swedish couple, parents of the owner, who had neglected to give them notice of the arrival of Flossie *et famille*. However, Nanny Herman, her mother, was enchanted after the first shock. It took her back to her girlhood in Norway, where she had grown up on a farm. Flossie and sister Lottie adjusted well to the simple farm life and throve. On returning to the city in the fall, the baby had gained a new lease on life.

This tough little mongrel settled again into her role of low man on the totem pole. Criticized by her mother, teased cruelly by her sister, pitied by her aunties, she had only her father, who would treat her as more or less a human fellow being. He thus formed a bond with the baby, inasmuch as he too was badgered by his wife, who was a dynamic, ruthless, money-hungry tyrant. But far from being put down, Flossie fortunately was very intelligent and almost precocious in her early development of speech, which, with her intense curiosity and social awareness, fended off any tendency there might have been to suffer depression and withdrawal.

As she grew in the shadow of her big sister, she nonetheless did very well in her scholastic endeavors, and when the family jumped over the Hudson to New Jersey, she was enrolled in a private school, commuting to Passaic daily on the Erie, where she attended The Collegiate School with her sister Charlotte, until in their teens they would enroll in the Gardner School in New York City. There she qualified for entrance to the sophomore year at Vassar, but her educational program was interrupted by her engagement to her future husband. She had observed this young doctor and fallen in love with him as he joined the swarm of admirers buzzing about her musical genius sister, and when he was rejected by Charlotte, he came running to Flossie, very much on the bounce. She was finally persuaded to accept his proposal of marriage out of love, or sympathy, or to establish her independence from her mother, in whose eyes the man was an odd versifier headed for certain penury. Her father again was her only ally. Her fiancé promptly took ship for Germany where he would study for eight months before returning to start his practice. Her suggestion of a career in nursing being ridiculed by her family, nursing supposedly being below her social status, and furthermore the physical demands (nursing in those days was *work*) would be much too strenuous! So she was left at loose ends, corresponding "periodically with her 'lover,'" and needling him with reports of some of her doings with her local rich beaus, precipitating great turmoil in the bosom of Bill Williams. But, after eight months, he would return to Rutherford, and the courtship was resumed on a day-to-day basis.

In another chapter I have outlined what in my opinion brought Flossie to accept his proposal of marriage.[2] Her position as the middle child, subordinate to her beautiful musician sister Charlotte, and outshone by the Nova on the Herman horizon, baby brother Paul, who would at least fill the role his mother sought: to return to Norway and reclaim the family estate. These considerations may in her own mind, at the ripe old age of 18 years, have left her with the specter of becoming an old maid, heaven forfend! Perhaps more challenging is the reasoning or instinct that led to Dad's proposal. Across the front of an envelope dated December 16, 1906, he had written, "[m]arriage is a disease, a sickness of the brain. What a crafty thing it is in the almighty that this love should turn our minds. Else who would marry, who in cold blood would marry if we were honest? There is no honesty about, the breed is dead!" And reviewing the 60 or so years of his awareness of women as desirable sexual playthings, I am impressed by one common denominator; the four who had the strongest influence over him, other than Floss, were all in some way involved with or actively participating in the arts.

In his college days in Philadelphia it was Hilda Doolittle (H.D., the poet) for whose attentions there would be friendly rivalry with Ezra Pound; during his internship, thanks to Ezra again, Viola Baxter Jordan came into his life with her interest in the art of writing, and her participation in minor parts at the Metropolitan Opera; back home, of course, was Charlotte Herman, a willowy beauty with rare talent as a pianist; and finally Madeleine Spence, again a talented musician. Was there a deep conservative vein flowing in the heart of WCW that warned him against his affinity for these artists? Was he aware, perhaps, of a need for a level head to rein in his sometimes hot one? Flossie certainly filled the role. Young, intelligent, well educated, well connected, attractive, no talent in the arts that might distract from her part as mother and homemaker, and to put the icing on the cake, she loved him.

With Floss, an added dimension was her father's wealth, which made possible the purchase of 9 Ridge Road, where my brother Paul and I were born in the first few years of their marriage. Mom was the brains of the outfit, while Dad brought home a modest income from his practice, whose management became one of Floss's most important duties. She was efficient, thrifty, industrious. I can't recall Mom taking a nap. She had a large circle of lady friends with whom she played bridge, and took up the game of golf at the old Yantakaw Club. The help, which was of varying quality, was taught and directed. She was impatient, like her father, of sloth and inefficiency. I can recall her cornering one of our maids in the kitchen closet, and having grasped her by the ears, or thereabouts, was bouncing her head off the wall, all the time berating her verbally for some *faux pas*. She tolerated Dad's friends in the arts up to a point, but when there began to be lice jumping on the furniture when they departed, they were no longer welcome in the house, and it became necessary for Dad's fellow travelers to meet in his office at the end of hours, perhaps to promote a loan.

Long gone the puny suckling. No longer functional the Herman family pecking order. Mom controlled the purse strings. Mom did the billing for Dad's practice, keeping a record of house and office calls at the desk and collecting and banking the receipts. Mom disciplined Paul and myself, which on occasion resulted in my going to bed with a wee nosebleed, Mom having interrupted a brotherly brouhaha over who got to go in the bath the first of a Saturday night. Callers at the front door were her responsibility, and she particularly recalled a person probably representing a local utility: "Good morning, lady," says he, "I would like to buy your house." "It's not for sale," says she. "Aw, come on, lady, everybody has his price," says he. "Okay," says Mom, "one hundred thousand dollars." "But lady, be reasonable," says he. Having bought the place for 8,000 dollars, it seemed a reasonable mark-up. "This is my home, and that's my price. Good day to you!" said she.

In the late twenties, Mom babysat Paul and I for a year while we were attending a private boys' school in Switzerland. She established her headquarters at the Hôtel-Pension des Familles, 14 rue de Lausanne, Geneva, just around the corner from the rue de Mont Blanc where was situated our favorite patisserie, hardly a block from the hotel. And just across the street from the railroad station, making it easy for us kids coming into town to meet Mom for Sunday dinner. I shall always remember the old lady at the foot of the stairway coming down from the station platform hawking her newspapers, "La Suisse, La Suisse!" in a husky baritone monotone.

Paul and I were originally enrolled at Coppet College, whence we took the train to visit Mom in Geneva. We later transferred to the Ecole Internationale in the town of Onex, west of Geneva. From there it was a short trolley ride into the city. It was here we met the Armstrong brothers, sons of Dad and Uncle Ed's school chum in the late nineteenth century.

Our departure from Coppet was largely due to Paul's serious illness with diphtheria, and Mom's battle with the school director, Monsieur Schwartz, over what she considered his inadequate treatment.

At the hotel Mom would leave her steamer trunk, stored for her when she was traveling, and returned to her room on her return. Here I learned to play bridge, Mom having purchased or borrowed a game called Auto-Bridge or some such. Here Paul and I would bring schoolmates for dinner, as reported in one of Flossie's letters to Dad.

> Did I tell you that the boys each invited a pal in to dinner Sunday. Bill invited Jean Brunel (son of the school's director), and Paul, a boy by the name of Philip Melness, whose father is the European representative for Paramount Pictures or some such company. Both boys were very sweet. Jean Brunel spoke fairly good English, but he and the boys talked French most of the time. Before dinner the kids consumed two pounds of cherries which I bought—then we had dinner. Then we went to the movies [all the Doug Fairbanks movies were being shown in Geneva] and had ice cream between the

acts. Then we went to tea and had more ice cream and patisseries. Then I dumped them on their tram and shipped them back to Onex.

Flossie always knew the way to a boy's heart was through his stomach.

But not all of Mom's experiences during our school year in Geneva were pleasurable. On one occasion it became her duty to accompany me to Juvenile Court, along with a classmate, Lucho Armstrong, a native of Uruguay, whose father had been a classmate of Dad's at the Chateau-de-Lancy in the 1890s. It seems Lucho and I had, with evil intent, pegged rocks at a streetlamp post outside the wall of the Chateau. Just like most American kids I had a pretty good wing, and it befell one of my missiles not only to smash the lamp, but further to bring it tumbling noisily down to the street, and it was our misfortune that the local gendarme, pedaling along the lane on his bicycle, witnessed the act. He sounded his whistle and gave chase. Lucho, being a much more accomplished escape artist than I, picked up the lamp, and with me close behind, we panicked and ran back into the school grounds. In retrospect it was a dead giveaway. We should have gone in the opposite direction, figuring he should never catch us if we stayed off the road. But all the cop had to do was go to Monsieur Brunel, the school director, and have us identified. All of which led to the aforementioned court appearance in the city, an ominous warning from the judge about the penalties for repeaters, and a considerable fine of about 80 Swiss francs.

Diphtheria struck the student body shortly after the beginning of the school year at Coppet, and brother Paul was among the sickest. Mom cabled Dad. Dad cabled Mom. Paul's progress was not up to Mom's expectations and she bugged the local doctor from Nyon, and the school director, to have a younger consultant or infectious disease specialist see Paul. She was reassured, in fact laughed at, but apparently her concern and criticism of his treatment resulted in her getting a call one evening at the hotel to the effect that Paul had been transferred to the infectious disease hospital in Geneva. This was the thirteenth day of his illness, and on the eleventh day she had examined Paul's throat herself, diagramming her finding on a copy of his clinical record and sending it to Dad. As the record shows, the kid's temp was rising again, and additional intensive care was called for. She was furious with the local doctor and the school for having presented her with a *fait accompli* without notifying her of Paul's transfer. But she felt obliged to modify the venting of spleen inasmuch as I was still enrolled at the school. Suffice it to say Floss went to the hospital, introduced herself, and transmitted Dad's cabled instructions to give massive doses of antitoxin. Paul staggered to a slow recovery and a prolonged convalescence. Like all of us who had the vaccine given to the whole student body at that place and time, he suffered giant hives recurring for weeks later.

The League of Nations was meeting in Geneva that fall, and Mom was an enthusiastic observer. In a letter to Dad dated September 27, 1927, she reports on the meeting of that date, stressing the popularity of the German delegate: "What a head Stresemann has! Ability shows all over him!"

> There is no doubt that the crowd comes to see the Huns, and you may well believe that they are worth looking at. All the other delegates speak either in French or English, but Herr Stresemann speaks German. I was told that the English objected quite strenuously at first, but were sat on by all the others, and with a very flowery speech the Japanese chief delegate informed the British that there are three world languages—English, French, and German. Hearty applause followed and the Kingfish had to retire, defeated. Today's session was interesting because everyone was there (except Lord Chamberlain). To hell with him anyway. I can see that a lot of good can be accomplished, merely by having all the different nations meet and be polite to each other—but England dominates the League. I also heard that England had sent several men over to US when the Republican Convention was on in Chicago—and through their influence and over a billion pounds, *not* dollars, Harding was nominated for President. They were sure that he could be persuaded to mess up matters so we would be forced to join the League—and it was a severe blow to Great Britain when Harding died. [...] I overheard two Britishers talking at the hotel yesterday, a group of legionnaires had just arrived, and one Britisher said to the other, "I haven't seen so much riff-raff on the continent since 1918."

And addressing herself to Dad's pro-ally prejudice: "That's what they think of you darling! Aren't they disgusting! And they *think* they are cultured and superior to us. They ought to be wiped off the face of the earth. [...] I'm sure that no other nation would speak of another in such a manner." An intelligent and efficient manager, yes. An observant and well-informed political commentator, indeed. An activist brooking no interference when she was convinced of her cause.

The community buzzed with rumors when Dad had returned from Europe alone, leaving Mom abroad alone for a year. Such an unprecedented action, at least in middle-class Rutherford. The marriage must be breaking up! But in retrospect, I can recall coming downstairs into the hall, shortly after our return from Europe, and observing Mom's skirt and petticoat rapidly ascending up about the hips as she and Dad met in the dining room, and her exclamation, "Oh Bill, not here!" and to complete the refutation of shoals ahead, I quote from a letter written in Geneva June 25, 1928, as we were preparing to sail back to the States:

> As to my feelings in regard to our marriage, I know it is *an extraordinary* success—but I have given up trying to put my reactions into words. I am very much like a cat, I think. I can quite contentedly sit back and purr when all goes well—and expect the world and all to see by my expression that they cannot equal my exalted position. I am rarely depressed—I am often angry—and then like a cat, I can scratch. Possibly I am primitive in my reactions. Yes, I guess that's it. But then the primitives were real people.

And in closing: "All my love, dearest baby.—I love you more and more all the time.—May the time fly until I see you. Yours, Florence." This may very well have been the happiest time of their married life. Earlier in the same letter Mom would write: "We may find ourselves over here [...] in some nice quiet spot writing famous novels and poems, etc., etc. Once the break has been made and the first book selling—and if it happens to go—you can never tell where it will lead to. At any rate it is something to think about." All this in anticipation of sales that never happened.

Irritated by what he considered inadequate advertising and printing of his work, Dad would leave New Directions, and sample McDowell-Obolensky, and later Random House, finally returning to Jim Laughlin at New Directions. Dad became resigned to his role of artist without a marker for his produce. Flossie's dream of withdrawal to a Shangri-La would never materialize.

Flossie returned to the United States at the time of the Great Depression. Who was buying poetry when many had trouble keeping bread on the table? Domestic economy was vital. I can recall Mom scolding Dad for standing at the sink with the water on full, waiting for a cold glass. Our socks were darned when there were holes. Our shirt cuffs and collars were turned when they became frayed. An itinerant tailor came into the house once a year, usually in the fall, and took the measurements of Dad, Paul, and myself, which went to a factory somewhere in Pennsylvania, and the finished products were delivered for a fitting some weeks later. Trousers were altered and patched when there was indication due to wear and growth.

Floss was a founder and active participant in the local co-op. No longer was she the lady of leisure doing the European Grand Tour! Flossie was forced to dig in. Dad's mother would come to live with us at 9 Ridge, and after a fall which made her a semi-invalid, she became a burdensome rival, demanding much of Dad's time and energy. They undertook to do a translation of a book from the Spanish, for example (which was not published until 1954).[3] And early in 1930, Mom's beloved father had suffered a fatal accident, killing himself with a shotgun not more than a few hundred feet from where the same fate befell his son Paul some years before.[4] I can recall walking down the hill from the big house to the well house with Dad and a group of men, police, etc., and seeing Poppops, as we called him, on the ground with a gaping hole through his clothing into his abdomen. Mom had stayed away. Dad cursed the gun, grabbed it by the barrel, and heaved it with all his strength out into the pasture, whence it was eagerly retrieved by one of the officers. Flossie's Dad lay under a blanket of red carnations, his favorite aroma, in the living room at 9 Ridge Road prior to burial in the local cemetery. Henceforth, Nanny (Mom's mother) was alone at the farm, depending on Floss for support and decisions of all kinds. We boys would go to help on weekends (I was driving by this time), doing chores, cutting and stacking wood for the kitchen range, weeding, running errands into town, etc. But the burden of the big house and the acreage became too much. Floss found her mother an apartment in Rutherford, and the whole kit and caboodle was auctioned off (a surprise finding was a 1921 Buick touring car which turned up when the farmer was removing the hay in the barn which he had purchased). So Nana Herman came back to town, and she too fell and fractured her hip, ending up in a nursing home in Ridgewood, where she lingered for some years.

There were escapes from the humdrum of Rutherford. One such was a steamer trip from Montreal to Newfoundland and Labrador, in August 1931, which gave Mom the opportunity to visit the post office in St. John's, and, with me in mind, to purchase blocks of stamps for my collection, some being older varieties dating back to the Cabot Issue of 1897, and later in the years of World War II, she would keep me current on the issues of the occupied countries.

Back at square one, we two kids, Paul and I, were demanding attention, jerking the leash in her left hand, even as Dad was pulling to the right. I would procrastinate my way through high school, much more concerned with fishing, soccer, and girls than the classic curriculum of college prep. With coaching in Latin, and irregular French verbs, I sneaked into Williams College. Paul, on the other hand, wasn't giving high school even lip service. As the principal, Dinty Moore, would say when approached for a letter of recommendation for college entrance, "Paul Williams played football at Rutherford High School." He in turn was farmed out to Mercersburg Academy, where because of his proficiency in swimming (Eastern Collegiate Swim Champ, 1937), he was prepped for admission to Dad's college, the University of Pennsylvania.

Mom kept her finger on us all through college, sending funds for our checking accounts, and in my case getting my laundry box of clean clothes back to school weekly (25 cents postage for a box of clothes, Rutherford to Williamstown). That old brown box with a rope running around side to side and front to back, quite often contained bonuses, like a batch of Lucy's brownies, a fifth of Mom's gin, concocted from grain alcohol stored in her bedroom closet (available during Prohibition on Dad's prescription for medical purposes), and occasionally a pill box of Cadalgia tablets, a favorite of my father's for subjective complaints like hangovers.

As soon as Paul and I made it through Harvard Business, and I through Cornell Med., Uncle Sam promptly snatched us. I was off to the South Pacific with the first detachment of Sea Bees.

The sparse stipend that a junior naval officer was paid was allotted to Flossie (who else?), and she squirreled it away in stocks and bonds, and on one occasion squandered a generous amount on a ring to be sent to the girl I left behind, then a Navy nurse. Dear Dotty. It was from her a couple of years later that I had my "Dear Bill" letter. Paul was off on destroyer patrol in the Atlantic and was no burden, having had the presence of mind to marry and produce a son before being tapped in turn by Uncle. His pittance as an ensign, USNR, would go to wife Ginny and son Paul. The war over, both Paul and I returned to Rutherford, he to begin a career in business with Abraham and Straus in Brooklyn, working up the chain to executive status and years later taking early retirement. I went back to New York Hospital to complete training in Pediatrics, and in 1948, when Dad had his first heart attack, I left my residency at NYH a few weeks early to take over the practice started by Dad in 1910.

This was the end of Dad's full-time medical career. He was from that time on more or less invalided and housebound at 9 Ridge. Mom was his full-time sitter, and would share with him the agonies of his illnesses, and his concerns about the publication of his work. Flossie also shared the psychological trauma of accusations by the "Red Hunters," Fulton Lewis, Jr., and Senator McCarthy. Particularly harmful was the yoyo experience of Dad's appointment to be Consultant in Poetry to the Library of Congress. Flossie got as far as locating an apartment for them in Washington, only to have the so-called investigation of his loyalty to his country, and further illness, wipe out any possibility of Dad 's accepting the post.

From the first myocardial infarct bringing a hospital bed to his bedroom, through surgery at New York Hospital for rectal malignancy, through repeated cerebral accidents and a two month stay at Hillside Hospital in Floral Park when his depression became profound, and throughout the terminal few years when his gait became awkward, his speech at times unintelligible, and his writing illegible, Flossie was there. Dad, meanwhile, continued writing, though at times he would discuss with Floss the idea of giving it up, because, as Mom told Win Scott in a letter, "[h]e thought nobody really cared about his writing."[5] Profits there were none, but he was being appreciated in literary circles away from academia, and Floss accompanied him on speaking tours from Puerto Rico to the West coast of the U.S., bracing and encouraging him through periods of despondency, particularly with the onset of the myocardial and cerebral thromboses, which with a bowel malignancy would eventually lead to his death. As Win Scott observed in a letter to Ben Bagdikian in 1955, "Floss is bright, sharp—right there beside him all the time, but never obtrusively, fussily so: just *there*."[6]

But as time went on, the accumulated traumas to her senses, the endless drains on her tolerance and patience would finally create a sore, a saddle sore if you will. "Asphodel" or no "Asphodel," the fact that she had been but one in her man's garland of roses would ultimately arouse her bile and precipitate verbal darts of venom. Particularly annoying were the *faux pas* at table, with food on chin, shirt and tie, in lap and on cuffs of sleeves. His outdoor booboos included leaving the hose running as his interest was diverted elsewhere, resulting in a merry little brook channeling its way across the yard, over the sidewalk and into the street. Mercifully, the driven, turbulent life of William Carlos Williams, hallmarked by his emotional spikes and troughs, ended in the early hours of

March 4, 1963. Mom called me shortly after dawn, and I went down to confirm his passing and console her.

There remained to Flossie 13 years of widowhood. For me the definitive image of Flossie in her last years is her enthronement on the couch in the living room at 9 Ridge, where she would bewail the passing of the *New York Herald Tribune*, settling for the *Times*; agonize over the departure of the Giants to San Francisco, making do with Brooklyn, and later the Mets; anathematize Nixon and Ike, and idolize Eleanor Roosevelt and Casey Stengel. During her last two years I was resident with her, as part of the ritual of procuring my divorce. We shared meal preparation, and ate together, and although I am no blue ribbon chef, she offered no criticism of my culinary efforts, other than an almost tearful request one Saturday noon as I brought her tray to the coffee cable in front of the couch: "Please Bill, could we have something besides cream of tomato soup and toasted cheese sandwiches?" It was an easy routine into which I had fallen, the quality and quantity of my calorie intake not being as important to me as to a shut-in, one of whose main pleasures is food! Not forgetting, of course, Stormy, her wonderful border collie companion.

Florence Williams. Photo by Musya Sokolova Sheeler, Irvington, New York, 1949. Courtesy the Poetry Collection of the University Libraries, University at Buffalo, The State University of New York.

These were busy years, marked by an active correspondence with, among others, Dorothy Pound, Marianne Moore, Bob McAlmon's sister, Victoria, Robert Lowell, Babette

Deutsch, Jim Laughlin, Sister Bernetta Quinn, Norman Holmes Pearson, Denise Levertov, Mary de Rachewitz, Tram Combs, Sculley Bradley, Neda Westlake, Theresa Abbott, Harriet Gratwick, Mary Barnard, Kay Boyle, Cid Corman, Gilbert Sorrentino, and many others. The biographers Reed Whittemore and Paul Mariani visited. Paul on many occasions staying the weekend. Also, Linda Wagner, Joel Conarroe, Hugh Kenner, M.L. Rosenthal, and countless other scholars and critics visited. Mary Ellen Solt, Jacqueline Ollier, and Sister Bernetta in the course of their respective studies would be houseguests. David Ignatow and Edith Heal interviewed her. Renewed friendship with Charlotte Earle led to the sisters joining in a nostalgic return to Alverheim, the ancestral manor of the Hafslunds, where Floss had visited as a child, followed by a cruise to the North Cape of Norway. Emily Mitchell Wallace became a warm companion, accompanying Mom on trips to the Greek islands and Nova Scotia.

As she lay dying in her bed at home, Paul and I sat with her one evening, she finally telling Paul to go home, he looked tired and had to work in the morning. I sat on for a while, and at her request brought her a glass of warm milk—she had complained of hunger. This she drank, and, apparently comforted, put her glass on the bedside table, closed her eyes and assured me she would be fine, and sent me in turn off to bed. When I came to wake her in the morning, she was gone, having died in her sleep.

Now, many years later, I am struck by the coincidence of the symbol of milk. As she lay critically ill in the first few days of her life, her father brought her milk, which comforted her and renewed her will to live. While I, her son, in the waning hours of that life, would bring her milk to solace her as the will to live expired.

from THE REWAKING (1962)

and so by
your love the very sun
itself is revived[7]

17

Summary

Family Doctor and Revolutionary Poet

> How do I long for a full expression of everything that is in me, a free outpouring of everything I feel. I have patience, I have love of men and women and children and trees—I can watch over a thing for years—in fact forever and nurse it into its full strength, but there is still a part of me that yearns for the unknown perfection—not a religious, heavenly perfection but a full-blooded earthly perfection that is fragile as all life is and as sweet.

Writing to his mother in the spring of 1916, my father sounds like anything but a struggling young physician, three years married, father of one and another child on the way, still being judged by the established physicians of the town, as well as a school doctor and physician to the county orphanage, serving gratis. In his freshman year at the University of Pennsylvania Medical School, he had established in his own mind that his love lay in the arts, but he would persist with his medical education for the income it would bring, thus making possible the pursuit of his muse. And his practice of medicine, like all things he would undertake would be a full-time job, conscientiously pursued, the needs of his patient always receiving first priority. As if to apologize to the art of medicine for placing it second to poetry, he would go to the front line in medicine, the trenches where the truly needy were, taking with him his knowledge and skill. He would become what we now know as a family practitioner.

This double commitment, to poetry and to medicine, would dictate his manner of living for the rest of his life. It demanded time and energy, and he would supply both bountifully, often at the expense of his family. Here at home we experienced a daily countdown and "blast off." By the time we assembled for breakfast, he had probably already done an hour's stint on the typewriter. There was no physicians' exchange—the phone was at his elbow at mealtimes. Another interruption was the mailman's whistle, announcing the morning delivery of mail. (A second delivery would come at one o'clock.) The list of calls having been compiled, he was out the door to the garage before we kids had swallowed our cod-liver oil and lit out for school. First stop probably the post office, mailing manuscripts and personal correspondence to maintain communication with his fellow poets, and in later years to advise the young ones aspiring to recognition. The house calls, working his way to the hospital for rounds, clinics, committee meetings, whatnot. Finally, home for lunch, a sit-down meal, hopefully 20 to 30 minutes allowed for nourishment and conversation with Floss. Often a quick nap on the couch in the living room, then one o'clock office hours, conducted for 40 years without a nurse or secretary assistance—a small attached lab for basic blood and urine analyses—one to three p.m., or until the last patient was seen. House calls again, particularly in winter, with perhaps 15 minutes swiped to get down a fragment of verse on the machine folded away beneath the office desk. Evening and supper waiting, Mom frequently telling Lucy, the maid, to put it on the table for herself and us two boys and a plate in the oven for the doctor. Home to eat. Napkin folded, rolled and tucked in its ring before retreat through the kitchen to the office again. Once more, hours seven to nine, or until the last patient was seen, hating this ultimate drain on his time and energy, as he would confess years later to Pound.[1]

Where in this hectic daily routine was there time for poetry? Where would he find energy and peace of mind to give "a free outpouring of everything I feel"? Where would he find "the unknown perfection—not a religious, heavenly perfection but a full-blooded earthly perfection that is fragile as all life is and as sweet?" Part of the answer lies in his great talent or genius for grasping or creating precious moments stolen from that alter ego, the doctor, and using them to unburden himself of poetic images. Perhaps on the road to the hospital, the car would be drawn to the curb and a fragment jotted awkwardly on a prescription pad or in a little red notebook that started life as a record of his doings as school doctor, and developed into a catchall for images, phrases, and poems.

Larger chunks of time were available while the rest of the world slept. It was at night that he would call on apparently endless stores of energy, the tattoo of his typewriter providing a reassuring lullaby to which my brother Paul and I slept and awoke throughout childhood. I can recall the projection of his mood brought to me by the cadence of the keys—the smooth *andante* when all was happy and serene, and the interrupted staccato when the going got rough, the carriage slamming, and the paper ripped from the roller, balled, and heaved in the direction of the wastebasket. Night was his time to roar. Here was happiness with his love, Poetry, but apparently in insufficient quantity or quality to completely satisfy. Further along in his letter to his mother he will say:

> I must do something [...] some high deed of spiritual happiness, nothing cowardly, nothing low, nothing small—some deed of great love for humanity perhaps, some venture for the sake of poetry, the art I love.

And in another paragraph:

> I must dare higher. It is only the fire we ourselves put into our lives that gives strength to our imaginations, it is the power of love that makes us live and do. Just as at Penn I gave up dentistry for medicine—just as a little later I really gave up medicine for poetry—and a little later I gave up a personal disappointment and its bitterness for dearest Flossie's love and the care of it, so now I feel on the brink of a new change.

Here is a man making his living at medicine who says he has given up medicine for poetry. One must wonder how the medical process, being an inexact science, could ever be a satisfactory medium for this man of strongly idealistic philosophy to employ in his search for the "unknown perfection," whatever that might be.

During his early and middle years he had frequently flirted with the idea of giving up medicine and seeking his living as a writer. Pound had urged him to pull up stakes and go to Europe, where the action was, and he and Floss made two trips to France, Austria, and Italy in the twenties, sampling the Bohemian life of the artists in Paris and living for a while on the Riviera. On their first trip in 1924, soon after World War I, they went to Vienna, where Dad studied in the clinics of what were then some of the leading lights in the beginning specialty of pediatrics. It was on his return to the States after this experience that he began to limit his practice more and more to the diseases of children. However, the dream of the artist's life never materialized. It must have been obvious to him that the public was not ready for his work: "Geeze, Doc, I guess it's alright / but what the hell does it mean?"[2] For which he had no answer, maintaining that if the poem had no significance to the reader on first reading, there was little hope that interpretation by the author would give any more profound enlightenment.

I recall a reading one evening at the home of a local physician, the audience consisting entirely of fellow doctors from his hospital. Gentlemen all. Fond of old Doctor Bill. Polite and attentive, aware of his reputation as a poet, anxious to get the word, i.e., the key to the code that would make it all clear. His closing lines were much in the form and mood of an orison:

O clemens! O pia! O dolcis!
Maria! Maria![3]

There was an appropriate silence at the conclusion, broken after ten or 15 seconds by the host, who inquired, "Are you a Catholic, Bill?" To which Dad replied in the negative, adding that so far as formal religion went, he was brought up Unitarian, though his parents had been Catholic and Church of England. It was immediately apparent to me that he was perturbed about something, although it wasn't until later driving home that he could explain his annoyance to me, i.e., the inference that his spontaneous expression of love and respect for some power beyond our understanding must stem from some formal catechism dictating his thought and emotions. However, there was nothing vindictive in his reaction, for by this stage in his life he had grown to accept his eccentricity and his designation as a revolutionary in the arts.

It was devastating to be rebuffed by his brother Ed.[4] Even more painful was the experience described in Chapter 4 of Dad's *Autobiography*:

> I'll never forget the dream I had a few days after he [his father] died, after a wasting illness, on Christmas Day, 1918. I saw him coming down a peculiar flight of exposed steps, steps I have since identified as those before the dais of Pontius Pilate in some well-known painting. But this was in a New York office building, Pop's office. He was bare-headed and had some business letters in his hand on which he was concentrating as he descended. I noticed him and with joy cried out, "Pop! So, you're *not* dead!" But he only looked up at me over his right shoulder and commented severely, "You know all that poetry you're writing. Well, it's no good." I was left speechless and woke trembling. I have never dreamed of him since.[5]

---

17. Summary

Misunderstood by the man in the street (whom he dearly loved), an enigma to his peers in the medical profession, condemned as a blasphemer by his closest pal, his brother, and, as they say in the vernacular, "wiped out" by his primogenitor, it becomes fairly obvious why he could never convince himself that there was a living for him to be made in writing. Fortunately, there was medicine, his *entrée* into the homes and minds of his neighbors, which qualified him to explore, as he himself put it, the ischio-rectal abscesses of mankind, and incidentally thereby earn a living. The "art" of medicine would be his crutch, supporting him and his family while he was "absent" on his crusade. How successful was his assault on the citadel only he would be qualified to say. Recognition by his contemporaries of a "good try" would come posthumously in the form of a Pulitzer Prize for *Pictures from Brueghel.*

APPENDIX

"My lullaby was my father's typewriter"

An Interview with William Eric Williams

RICHARD P. QUATRONE

Recorded on October 16, 1980, at 9 Ridge Road, Rutherford, New Jersey. Transcript revised August 1981.

Introduction

On October 16, 1980, I drove down Ridge Road. The same street I'd driven down so many times since I'd first learned how to drive years ago, but this time I was paying a visit to number 9. It was odd to think that I'd passed this house hundreds of times in my youth with no knowledge of William Carlos Williams who was still alive and writing in the house which sits at the edge of Rutherford's business district. In fact, 9 Ridge Road is the very first residence on the road which extends through Rutherford, into Lyndhurst (where I'd lived as a teenager), through north Aldington, and into Kearny and Harrison, where the name becomes Kearny Avenue. This road was always the "main drag" for me as a teenager who, like so many other restless, bored kids, "drove Ridge Road" over and over again looking for some kind of undefined excitement which was so sorely lacking in the towns we lived in.

I was nervous enough to arrive several minutes late for my scheduled

7:30 appointment with William Eric Williams, the eldest son of the poet. Mrs. Williams greeted me at the door and guided me into the living room where Dr. Williams was standing, hands in pockets, waiting for me. We greeted one another, and he immediately asked me where I was from originally. Even as we were making ourselves comfortable in soft, living room chairs, the doctor began talking about his father's publisher, James Laughlin of New Directions. Dr. Williams seemed pregnant with information and needed no prodding from me to talk. I managed to turn on my cassette recorder somewhere into the doctor's discourse, and the interview officially began.

The interview ended with this same spontaneity. In a real sense it never began or ended. My recorder was simply turned on and turned off. The doctor apparently welcomed this opportunity to talk and to share his feelings and thoughts. He seemed to enjoy the contact immensely. Later in the evening, he took me on a casual tour of the downstairs portion of the house. He showed me his office and examining rooms, and he explained where his father had practiced and how some of the rooms had been changed over the years since his father's death.

Perhaps the richest part of the evening occurred as the doctor and I sat in the kitchen drinking canned soda and discussing freely everything from politics, teaching, raising a family, to modern medicine and modern poetry. I recall thinking to myself how I'd wished this was on tape. The doctor asked me if I had to go to work the next day. I responded I did, and we were both reminded of the limitations of time and place. My feeling was that we could have talked half the night.

As it was, Dr. Williams walked me through the house, out the front door, and down the front walk to the sidewalk. It was an unusually warm night for mid–October, and, as we stood exchanging friendly words of parting, I remember thinking how quiet Ridge Road had become.

Richard P. Quatrone
Passaic, New Jersey
August 1981.

Richard P. Quatrone *is a poet and playwright who co-founded and edited* Passaic Review *in 1979. He participated in the New Jersey Poetry Renaissance of that time and was an officer in the New Jersey Poetry Society.*

* * *

WEW: I think all of his life Dad would have liked like hell to forget his medicine and devote his life to his art.

RPQ: That's a question I was going to ask you.

WEW: He came on a hell of a dilemma, and he fought it I'm sure for many, many years. He would have liked very much to have turned his life completely into writing. So, there were a lot of facets to the guy. But then he was married to a very practical gal, my mother. And he had two kids and a war and a Depression. So, he stuck with medicine as his bread and butter, and he used his art as his escape and his relaxation. The characteristic of my father was his fantastic energy. Everybody'd say, how the hell did he do it? How did he do all that? Make a living, deliver over a thousand babies and still write 40 books, or however many books it was. He was a guy who could come in here on the couch and plop. Mom would get him up and into the office.

RPQ: TV wasn't a big factor.

WEW: Aaaacchh.... TV was zero. Radio, television, the media, he had no use for them. He'd read, he and Mom, read, she'd read to him or he'd read to her. They did a lot of crossword puzzles. They were a good partnership.

RPQ: One of the articles I read was printed either by the University of Pennsylvania or another non-literary source. And the question in this article was how did he find the time to do the creating. His answer was it's not how you find the time but what you do with the time. Which is very true.

WEW: As he said in his famous line, when the patient stepped out, the typewriter popped out.

RPQ: He must have been very intense.

WEW: Yes, he was very intense. Yes. And yet my brother and I have always laughed at the image that he presented as he walked from the house to the garage going to the hospital or something: his coat was open, his hat was half-assed on his head, his bag was in his hand, and he habitually performed an atonal whistling between his teeth [whistles]. It's a little standard joke my brother and I have, now he'd sort of stare off into space [whistles again]. That's Dad. His mind was far away. Ostensibly he was on his way to save a life, but actually he was thinking bigger things. He was a character. Yeah, he was an intense guy, but fortunately he had energy. And, as I've often said, my lullaby was my father's typewriter. He was bangin' away long after I got to sleep, and he was bangin' away when I woke up in the morning. He was at it again! He was very, very intense. He got onto a thing and worried it until he got it.

RPQ: He didn't really relax when he wrote.

WEW: He was always a two-fingered typist [humorously mimicking typewriter sound]. Then he hesitated, then zzzzzzzip! ... [humorous sound again] ... zzzzzzzzzzzzzip! Another sheet of paper, you know. Yeah, he was always thinking. And a little tragedy: he had a favorite nurse up at Passaic General Hospital, which was his hospital, and sometimes in the morning after his early house calls, like the milkman, he'd get up to the hospital, and somewhere along the line he'd have a flash. And he'd get to the hospital and say, "Annie, Annie Oley, put this with the rest." She had a file. And goddammit that thing was lost or destroyed or stolen. It was shortly after Dad died. I asked her what happened to it, to all the poems. I said, "Annie, I don't want them, but they are valuable for you and for the world." I mean, these were works of art. And she was embarrassed. She was such a conscientious, lovely person from the Passaic area. They were completely kaput.

RPQ: These were poems that have never seen publication?

WEW: Never published, never. It was sad. Too bad. He was always bangin' things out, I've come across a few things around the house, come across some, you know, when you use carbon paper instead of running it through a copier. He would use carbon. I found carbons with original works on them that hadn't been typed on too much. I'd pick it up and send them to his publisher. See if they could pick up anything from it. But there's not much that hasn't been published, as far as I know.

RPQ: I was really interested to hear you say that you've written essays and have had some published.[1]

WEW: Yes, little things. I wrote about characteristics of his, the way he handled a car.

RPQ: Off the top of your head?

WEW: Yes, yes.

RPQ: What about memoirs per se? Are those the memoirs that Denise Levertov refers to?

WEW: Oh, I suppose so. It's just little things. I was encouraged to do it. I didn't know how to start, so I thought what's important is a man's life? His home. So, I took the house. I did this [pointing in the living room], and I did the perspective from the windows here, what you see, characteristics of the house and grounds. He was a great guy for the physical senses. Smell, taste, hearing. He enjoyed music. He enjoyed food. So, I did one on food.

RPQ: I'm going to have to get this.

WEW: Oh, it's around here somewhere. Oh, what's her name, the girl at Penn State insisted I copyright it.[2] I copyrighted one but I haven't got around to the others. I'll show them to you, I hope.

RPQ: Which has actually taken away the need for my asking if your dad ever encouraged you or your brother to be an artist to be a writer. Did he ever directly encourage you?

WEW: None whatsoever. If anything, he was a negative influence because I think he felt very strongly that.... I think he realized towards the end of his life, when he began to realize he was famous.... He never thought he would be. He poo-pooed the whole thing. That's why he stuck to medicine rather than to art. And, uh, he even kind of talked down medicine. We weren't influenced strongly by him one way or the other. I think I was influenced to go into medicine because of the community. You know, you're Dr. Williams's son. You're gonna major in chemistry and biology and you're gonna be a doctor. You took six years of Latin, and this and that and the other thing. You don't take what these other kids take. It was funny.

RPQ: How about your brother?

WEW: My kid brother, he had also started out as pre-med down at Penn, and I think he got to the second year and turned it in.

RPQ: Then he went into business?

WEW: He went into business administration. He just took a straight arts degree at UPenn. Then he went up to Boston, at Harvard, went to Harvard for business administration. Yeah, he couldn't take the sciences.

RPQ: I was wondering, if you had to say what was the most unique effect of being raised by a man who was so creative, a poet, as opposed to bring raised by just any other type of man, would you say there were any particular burdens, or any particular joys, for you? What was it like?

WEW: Uh, I'll tell you, while it was going on, while the growing up was going on, uhm, there was very little relationship with our father. My brother related better than I did. Uh, I had a very, uhm, wispy relationship with dad. Uhm, I think he was very much concerned in, again, in an intellectual kind of way about his boys. What was gonna become of them, what they were, what they were gonna become. But uhm, he was so occupied with his business, his medicine and his vocation, avocation, or whatever—the writing, that there was very little time left for anything else. I mean, physical energy, emotional energy. Christ, how much can one guy do in a lifetime, how can he emote on his poetry, emote on his kids, emote on his wife, emote on his practice, good God! No, he, uh, as an adult—if anyone ever becomes an adult—as a so-called adult, in retrospect, looking back, I think my father had a very negative influence on me as a growing up kid. Uh, I turned to things that he really wasn't concerned about. I became an avid fisherman.

RPQ: Yes, I've heard that.

WEW: And I found an adult, male patient of my father's who was a fisherman, and I latched onto that guy like a bloodsucker. And he dragged me through, uh, I guess from 13 to 18, four or six years, in the teens there, which are very important years for a young man growing up. The formative years in the father-son relationship are very important.

RPQ: So, your dad really wasn't there for you.

WEW: Dad wasn't there. Dad was there for Dad. To support his art. When he got a free moment, or a free hour, he was in the library reading for "Paterson," or he was in New York editing *Contact* or some mag that he was particularly interested in, or down in Greenwich Village.[3] I remember occasionally going with him on a Friday and being stuck in a corner, and they'd be beatin' their gums, all over my head, being given an orange, here peel it, and what went on around me I wasn't aware of.

RPQ: And then there was the time, for instance, I think it was in 1927 or 1928 when you and your brother and your mom were in Europe, separated for a whole year from your dad.

WEW: [Coughs] There we were. [Long silence]

RPQ: So, uh, well, would you say that, uh, what was I going to say. Would you say that it was more of a blessing or a burden having a father who was a poet? It sounds like more of a burden from a child's point of view, from a young man's point of view.

WEW: From a child's point of view, sure. Later on, I can remember as a junior in college, a sophomore or a freshman, what the hell ever it was, at lunch one day during the finals in June.... May, June ... whatever it was, one of the seniors had just come into lunch from his English exam, and he said, "Jesus Christ, did anybody ever hear of William Carlos Williams!" You know [laughing]. "Yeeeeeah! That's my Pop!" He says, "Jesus Christ, I failed that. Never heard of him!" Anyway, he was a question on a Williams College English exam in 1933, '34, something around there. I think that was probably one of the first times that my father turned out to be a prestigious figure, you know, in my life. What the hell, I knew he was a doctor, I knew he was respected, I knew that he wrote and he had a helluva lot of queer friends. After all, the art world is full of quote unquote "queer" people—off people, people who don't fit in the standard mold, not necessarily their sexuality or their lack of sexuality, or their, uh, what am I trying to say ... their intellectual characteristics, whether they were labored intellectuals or spontaneous intellectuals.

RPQ: How did you father fit in with these people? I seems like a lot of people were coming here.

WEW: Oh, he fit in with anybody!

RPQ: Yet, he was the established physician, and a lot of these guys probably didn't even have jobs.

WEW: That's right. They'd come out here and bum five dollars. They'd show up in the office and hang around the waiting room until he was through. They wouldn't dare come in here [referring to the house proper]. Mom would have killed them. "Bill, old buddy." They couldn't come in here. They left lice on the furniture. It was interesting.

And they fought, Mom and Dad. It was a tough life, for her too. But, because of his absent-mindedness, his mental devotion to his vocation and his profession left the practical side of his life completely neglected. If it hadn't been for Mom! She had to grab him by the collar, "For Christ's sake, sit down! Where the hell have you been today? What did you do? Who did you see? How much, what's the charge?" You know, who paid, who didn't? And he'd go around his pockets, and he'll pull out some money and checks and stuff, and she'd say, "Now, who gave you this?" "Well, let's see." And she used to sit over there at the desk and had a little bookkeeping system that they kept together. He was absolutely unconcerned about the buck, you know.

RPQ: It's kind of a loaded question, but how was he with charging his patients? How was he with the managerial side of being a doctor?

WEW: Terrible! He never had an assistant or aide in his office. He was that kind of guy. He worked alone. And when I came in with him and came into the office and brought a nurse, ah, he didn't know how to act [laughs] in the office. In the hospital, of course, in the delivery room, the operating room, anywhere in the hospital he worked, on the floor, in the wards, with patients and nurses, of course he knew how to act. But in his own little sanctuary that he had out here, that was his own *sanctum sanctorum*. There he did his own thing, his own way. And it wasn't colored or tempered by the presence of anyone else. It was strictly one on one. And since he's died, uh, I see people, of course, who knew him.

RPQ: You still have your practice here?

WEW: Yes, right here. But many people remember him as kids. My generation, or a generation of half generation behind me say, "Gee, Doc, your father, he was a great guy. Boy, when I was sick, and I had this terrible thing, and my mother had this and that ... you know, he never sent us a bill." A funny thing, before mother died in '76, a letter came in the mail out of the blue one day asking for a bill for service he had rendered 20 or 30 years before. He'd delivered a baby, and the family had moved away and never paid him. Well, they were conscience stricken. They lived down in Florida. They asked mother what was the fee. Of course, nowadays it would cost them a thousand dollars. Mom sent them a bill in one of dad's old billheads we had kicking around here for 50 dollars. But so many people said, oh God, your father was.... You know, the public loved this: a guy who gives them all the care and doesn't send them a bill [laughs].

RPQ: Oh sure. I mean, I'm not a doctor, and I think he sounded like a great guy! [both laughing]

WEW: Well, that's the image.

RPQ: Of course, to another physician he probably sounded like he was a little crazy, you know. Or to another business man.

WEW: When I first came into practice here, it wasn't easy. Because I was practicing in the same office, and I was taking over his practice after the war. I came back in '46, went to New York, took postgraduate training in New York a couple of years. Then I came out to practice with him. And he had ill health: heart problems, a couple of strokes. One thing, at least when I went to medical school, you don't learn a damn thing about the practical side of medicine: how much to charge and so on. And I still didn't know, you know. Hell, I was out of medical school, I left school, I was the class of '40, I'd been in medical school since '36, and here it was 1948! I'd been through medical school, internship, residency, the war, and back to New York with two more years special training in pediatrics, and I had never earned a buck! Except in the navy where you get paid automatically. Occasionally in New York, when I did a special favor for one of the private attendants, he'd send me a check for ten bucks or something like that. And of all the people in the world to teach a young doctor the value of his services, my father was ridiculous! [laughs] He'd take care of newborn babies in the hospital and, because they were his patients, he never sent them a bill. No charge. I started out in pediatrics, these were my bread and butter, and I wasn't charging them because my dad said, "Ah, I never like to charge these people because, after all, I know the husband...."

RPQ: And he tried to pass this on to you? The influence?

WEW: [Somewhat annoyed] He didn't try to pass anything on to me. It was just that he was senior, you know, they guy around here. And this was the image, the only image I had to imitate. What the hell, I didn't know anything about the private side of practice.

RPQ: You know what Whittemore calls this in the Poet from Jersey *book? He calls it the "humanistic tradition" that your father adheres to.*[4]

WEW: Well, whatever it was, he sure adhered to it. [slightly resigned]. But, gradually I broke away from that. He'd flip if he came back to life one week to see all the non-services that doctors pawn off on patients and get rich off. It stinks.

RPQ: A different question. I was going to ask you, do you have a favorite work?

WEW: Yes, "Yachts." These have, ah, sociologic overtones. It gets me, on this sort of thing I'm with him. A lot of his things, they leave me at home plate. I think he was a hell of a good doctor. I think, in my opinion, ah, he was the best doctor around here. And, uh, he had the qualities of a good doctor. He had the knowledge of a physician. A physician needs a good, basic knowledge. He had a fantastic knowledge of anatomy, knew things you don't use for years. He was a good doctor, a good diagnostician. Another thing that made him a very good doctor was his patient relationships. They were very warm. Even in his lifetime, the image that a physician had created, even till the time I'd come around, was the family doctor, the friend, the fellow you could call anytime day or night, who could relate to you on a first name basis. It was very nice. And then there was the kind of person who wanted the doctor to be a, uh, uh, a figure head....

RPQ: A god.

WEW: ... a god, symbol, a thing, a cold, very efficient, business-like man, neatly dressed, with a little mustache and a monocle ..., and Dad, he was the first kind. He was an old-fashioned doctor, but still he was sharp, very sharp. Another thing I liked about him was the way he knew his patients. He didn't kid anyone. So many doctors, they'll drag a patient along for a long time, and make a good living on it, until suddenly the patient realizes he isn't getting anywhere, and he's failing or dying, then he goes some place else. Dad, if he had a patient and knew there was something seriously wrong with them, he could pin it within the system—the nervous system, the cardiovascular system, the renal system, the musculoskeletal system. But if he should fail, in a small percentage of cases, to be able to exactly pinpoint where the problem was, he didn't hesitate to get a consultation. "There are guys who are much more knowledgeable than I, and you deserve a second opinion."

RPQ: He was very honest.

WEW: He was extremely honest. That was his most painful quality. Holy Jesus, he was honest.

RPQ: That could have had something to do with his being a poet. Since that's one of the qualities of a lot of poets, a painful honesty. You wish they'd go away sometimes. You know, you don't want to hear the truth all the time. Let me ask you this: I had some confusion in my mind, when we did the reading at 131,[5] I was under the impression that your dad was born there.

WEW: No, down the street a few doors.

RPQ: Okay, because on page nine of the Whittemore book, when I read it I was surprised. He said your dad was born in a place that no longer stands. It was down the street?

WEW: It's still there. It's a little skinny house about two doors from the corner. I think Mariani will get all these little details right. You know, some years ago they made a movie using me as my father. I was the actor. It was made here in Rutherford. They came, moved into my home with cameras and lights and technicians and all that crap.[6]

RPQ: What happened?

WEW: It's on file somewhere at an educational film place at the University of Michigan.

RPQ: I thought you meant a regular film for television.

WEW: It was, it was!

RPQ: I've never heard of it. Has it been....

WEW: Well, who cares? [annoyed] But anyway, it was made.

RPQ: It sounds like something worth seeing.

WEW: You can get it out, I'm sure. A guy who's very knowledgeable about these things, about my father, is Fred Martin, who is Jim Laughlin's right-hand man, and of course the girl who did the bibliography[7]—she's the most knowledgeable person of all about his works.

RPQ: Edith Heal?

WEW: No, no, the bibliography.

RPQ: Hoagland?

WEW: No, not her. But Kitty is an old friend. Her husband was a good newspaper man.

RPQ: Is she still around?

WEW: To the best of my knowledge she's still around. So is her husband. So, the question was ...?

RPQ: The question was, where was he born?

WEW: He was born on West Passaic Avenue. But not at 131. Further down the block. A lower number.

RPQ: All right. But I'll tell you, there was something I was reading about, I read it twice to be sure that I had it in my mind. It was a painful time. It was upsetting to read it, so I can only imagine what it was like to go through. I don't know if you want to comment on this: it was the affair with the Library of Congress, which was right after you started practicing over here.

WEW: Yes.

RPQ: I got the impression that this guy Luther Evans and whoever else was in charge down in Washington really did a number on your father, raising certain questions about his reputation, and then leaving him out on a limb. And my question is, specifically, would you say that that was the worst crisis in your father's life?

WEW: It really hurt him. Mom and Dad were all set to go, you know, to the point of finding a place to live, ready to close up here and go, that sort of thing. It was a mean blow. It hurt him a lot. Uh, I've never heard anybody comment on what it did as far as his work, his writing, his creating, ah, from that time on, but I think it certainly must have had a tough effect on him.

RPQ: Even creatively you think it may have diminished his work?

WEW: Creatively, definitely, definitely. Because it came at a time in his life, ah, when everything was coming to an apex, to a peak, in a way, yet he was beginning, intellectually, physically, he was beginning to deteriorate. A time in his life when, gee, if something good had happened, if something, a job like that, if he'd had the opportunity, had the urge, given the ... [snapping fingers searching for words]

RPQ: Recognition.

WEW: No, no, not recognition, but given the incentive, given the incentive to go on being a creative person, being a poet, being an American influence, image, ah, promoter, and he was, he was all of that.... If that stupid Library of Congress thing hadn't been happened, I think the last years of his life would have been an awful lot happier. It would have given him, as I said, the incentive to go on. As it was, you know, it took the top off of it. A terrible leveler. And from there on it was a matter of ill health.

RPQ: Would you say that had a lot to do with the ill health? Or was it mostly incidental?

WEW: The more we learn about the psyche, sure. I think that the psychosomatic influences were tremendous on his life. Whether in positive or negative ways, I mean, a woman has three little kids and she's dying of Hodgkins disease grits her teeth and says goddamit, I'm not going to die for 15 years until I get these kids out of their diapers. And so forth and so on. Given dad, with great anticipation, it would have been ah, ah, a wonderful thing for the two of them together. God knows, they'd had a little enough time, really, you know, day in and day out living together. This would have been wonderful. Then to have it just cut out from under him [snap his fingers] ... screw you, bub!

RPQ: I read that, uh, 20 years later, uh, the Library of Congress published an anthology of poets who had served as consultants, and your father was listed with an asterisk saying that he had not served. But evidently they considered him to have been appointed, which is all very nebulous. You know, it doesn't make much sense. Who can explain that kind of reversal, whatever the motivations? Even reading about it twice, I never really....

WEW: People are always asking me about his illnesses: when did he have this illness, when did he have that illness, how did it affect his writing after that, what did it do to his last, uh, and you know he changed so, uh, what am I trying to say? Anyway, I think it's obvious, after the Library of Congress thing, everything was downhill. Or course, there was an abrupt change. It was a tragic change. Well, it isn't painful for me, but it was certainly painful for him.

RPQ: Do you have a daughter?

WEW: Four of them.

RPQ: Do you have one called Emily?

WEW: Yep.

RPQ: From what I know, I don't know much about her, but am I right to assume that she is a poet in her own right? She writes poetry?

WEW: She likes to write poetry.

RPQ: Was she, ah, I noticed that your dad had a grandmother by the name of Emily Dickinson Wellcome. Was that her namesake?

WEW: Emily Dickinson, right. I named Emily after my father's grandmother, yes.

RPQ: Just interested in knowing.

WEW: Emily Barrett Williams. That's her name.

RPQ: She's got quite a namesake to try to live up to. [laughs]

WEW: They're all family names. Emily will soon be 30.

RPQ: I didn't know she was that old. I don't know much about her, I've heard about her, if this is the same person. I've heard people at Fairleigh

Dickinson mention that she writes. I've seen her stuff in local magazines a few years ago. I thought she was a lot younger than she is.

WEW: No. My baby is 18. The next is 23, 22, 23, and the next one is 26–29, 26, 23, and 18.

RPQ: You mention people asking you about your father's health and so on. Do poets still get in touch with you? You know, are people in the literary world, aside from some of the publishers that you deal with, the average poet like myself....

WEW: They come from the damndest places. I mean I've gotten letters....

RPQ: They knock on your door? I mean what do they do? What happens?

WEW: Well, on Thursday or Friday there was a guy working here, preparing a wall. My wife was out, and I was in the office. And he came in.... Hey Doc, there's a guy here from Germany to see you [laughs]. This guy and his wife came over from a German university, they're in New York, and he's a William Carlos Williams scholar. So you come out and you talk. And the next guy or woman, may be the head of a woman's poetry club from Spring Valley, New York. She stops in. Her husband is a salesman who sells needlepoint. He leaves needlepoint samples here because he's so grateful. She wants to read to the woman's club up across the state line. I have letters. I can't answer them, from local scholars, from colleges. A guy from New Zealand popped in. A guy from London popped in. Another from Nice, France. An English professor at University of Zurich came by.

RPQ: What do they assume that you have? Do they come for scholarly information? What are they looking for?

WEW: Well, no, they're looking ... as you came in, they notice a sort of halo, they want to come feel the aura. They want to get a little of the, uh ... and take it back home with them. [Laughing] I was there, and "I know," you know. And lots of them have specific questions. A lot of them write me letters, people trying to do a paper, and they want you to write it for them. Three or four typed pages, with long questions in one paragraph, and they'd leave two paragraphs where you could fill it in. That kind of crap. Mother would get furious. Take the goddamned thing and throw it out! It was stupid.

RPQ: Do you feel, then, have you felt your privacy in any way invaded?

WEW: Oh, sure, to some extent. But it's been all my life, so I'm used to it now. My poor wife, she's my wife for four years, it's been a new experience for her. But she's getting the message, now, too, you know. That's the way it is. It's good and bad.

RPQ: I'll tell you, when I thought about doing this interview, early on, looking for a focus, I decided it wouldn't be right only to look for information about your father. I really felt that the interview, as much as I could make it so, should focus to a large extent on you, as the son of a person who had such and such a background, you know, how it has affected you, what your feelings are, what your perspectives are. Ahm, I didn't come to see you as, I didn't expect that you would be scholarly, ah, critic of your father. I didn't expect that.

WEW: I am not. I am not a knowledgeable scholar about my father.

RPQ: I don't think that would be the value of talking to you. I think it would be right to hear what you had to say from your point of view.

WEW: Right.

RPQ: For instance, you were talking about the kind of absence you felt, you know, as you were growing up. With the thing with your dad.

WEW: It was very real.

RPQ: I worry, in my own life, because, I don't have children yet, but I don't even know how I would. One of the things I worry is that, ah, I don't know what kind of father I would be. I'd love my children. But I often think how I'd have to cut into my other interests. It's difficult to have two different careers, in effect, and then to have your friendships. And to carry on normal, mundane activities of living. I read somewhere, this might be hard, I don't know if it's a question; I read that somewhere, a comment, but I don't know which card it's on, these damn cards, that you had a kind of love-hate relationship with your dad. That was in the Whittemore book, too, I think. Was there ever a major conflict? What would have been a point of contention? Was it a normal conflict between a father and son? There are always conflicts between sons and fathers. I had terrible fights with my father before he died.

WEW: Sure. The old Oedipal complex, trying to resolve your rivalry for the old lady in the house.

RPQ: The traditional kind of thing? Nothing exceptional?

RPQ: She really raised you....

WEW: Oh, yes. Yes. I mean, when you had a question, you didn't go to Dad, for God's sake, you went to mother. For your allowance, a clean pair of socks, do I have to do my homework, or whatever the hell it was. You went to Mom. I mean, ah, Dad passed through the room, you know ... [whistling]

RPQ: Oh, God! [both laugh]

WEW: Headed for the typewriter.

RPQ: [Laughing] Sounds very funny, but I'm sure it wasn't.

WEW: What the hell! He was on cloud nine. Absolutely! That's where he lived when he wasn't in his clinic.

RPQ: So, your mother, I'm getting the impression that your mother was a very independent woman.

WEW: Mom was a strong person, fortunately. Yes, she was.

RPQ: She had a lot of interests which did not include your dad. In other words, she developed things for herself....

WEW: She had to. She had to.

RPQ: The women's liberationists would probably find her to be the paradigm, being to stand on her own....

WEW: Nah, I think she'd poo-poo it, or I think she'd say this is a lot of BS. I think Mother's attitude would have been, for god's sake, if they weren't gutsy enough to get what they thought was coming to them without having to go through all this hoop-dee-do, what the hell good are they? It's all artificial. Because she got what she wanted without all this political nonsense.

RPQ: All this structure to work with.

WEW: Goddamned right! She was a strong one. She was a good one. Tough.

RPQ: I have a quote here. This is from the Foreword to the autobiography, in which your dad says, this is pretty much an exact quote: "What I believe to be the hidden core of my life will not easily be deciphered, even when I tell, as here, the outer circumstance."[8] And my question for you is, did you ever know, or your mother, or your brother, did you ever get to know the "hidden core" of your father?

WEW: No. I don't think so. I don't think so. And I don't know if at any time in my life I was closer to it than at any other time.

RPQ: How about your mom?

WEW: I don't know. I think my father was an enigma to my mother till the time he died. I don't think that Mom really, whether it was disappointment, whether she stopped wondering after a while, her curiosity died, or whether it was something that was intellectually or physically beyond her ability to grab, to comprehend. I don't know. I just don't know. And I've had questions like this from many people. A doctor, a Rutherford boy, Stanley Koehler went through high school, and then in Massachusetts too, and he asked me some rather profound questions about my father and about his influences, what was in his library. Whether he'd ever read Freud, whether he'd ever read this, that, or the other thing. I don't know. I don't know. Can't answer it.

RPQ: His library's at Fairleigh Dickinson.

WEW: Some of it.

RPQ: I've seen what they have of it over there.

WEW: I don't know. I've thought that, if I'm going to go on with this series of essays, sketches, I should be able to talk around that point, or talk, drop some relevant pearls about that facet, yet I just don't know if I'd be able to. I don't know. But, I'd like to. It would be fun. Everything I've written has been surface stuff, nothing really about the man, about his mind or emotions, just the physical things, the somatic man, his physical nature.

RPQ: How many essays have you written, off hand?

WEW: I don't know. Not much. There or four.... Let's see ... the house, the food, the car.

RPQ: That's interesting. I think he would have understood that type of thing.

WEW: I guess I was probably influenced, when I started to write, by him. Let's see, what would he have said? What else did I have to copy?

RPQ: He said "no ideas but in things."[9]

WEW: That's right. I put all the things down. His hat size, his shoe size, how much butter he ate. I think it's relevant. And one of the things, it's funny, at the time I started to knock off these little papers, I was in a streak of reading biographies of Frenchmen. I was reading Renoir. I was reading Gauguin, Toulouse-Lautrec, etc. I had read Renoir's story of his father, and when I got through the book, I was dissatisfied because there was no physical picture of the man. There was lot of stuff about where he went, where he lived, how he got there, how he got back, who his friends and influences were, but I had no physical picture, and to me, maybe it's because of my training in anatomy, you've got to have the thing there to work on. I had no image of the man at all. I didn't know who they were talking about. They could have been talking about the chair, as he went to Paris, or whatever he did; and I said, Jesus, nobody else has done this either, and in my little corner I'll knock off a physical picture, and if anybody really wants to know what the old boy looked like, he can turn to my little sketches. So, that got me started.

RPQ: I saw something somewhere, according to what you had written, somewhere your name was mentioned, father is five feet nine, he had the same shirt size I have, 15½ two sleeve, I have a short arm.

WEW: I do too.

RPQ: And I said this to my wife. She said I should ask you if you have any shirts.

WEW: He had an 8-D shoe, 36 to 38 jacket. He never weighed over 165.

RPQ: Thirty-two, 34 waist I recall reading. Those were your notations?

WEW: Yes.

RPQ: Very interesting.

WEW: I thought that was necessary. If you want to remember a guy, and he's that famous, they probably don't even have a good physical picture of Napoleon or Alexander the Great—but, by God, for my Pop they're going to have a pretty good picture, you know.

RPQ: He's shorter than I imagined him.

WEW: He wasn't a big man. A terrible temper, though. He'd blow his stack! His brother was a hell of a batter. He was an architecture student at MIT. Summertime he played semi-pro ball. It helped pay for school.

RPQ: He must have been pretty good.

WEW: He was good. A catcher. And he could hit any of the locals when they played here with the church. He could straighten out anything they threw at him. And this one pitcher got mad as hell, threw a beanball at him.[10] My dad went out and was down the pitcher's throat. He wanted to kill him.

RPQ: Where was this?
WEW: In a local field.

RPQ: This field is no longer here?
WEW: Oh, yes, it's here, but they changed the name of it. Yes, he loved to play ball. Ed's now dead. That's one of his paintings over there. That's a church right up there on Route 46.

RPQ: Your uncle.
WEW: Yes.

RPQ: I knew he was an architect, but I didn't know he was a painter.
WEW: That was his hobby. That's his mother's painting right over there in the corner. She painted the portrait near the bookcase. That's her work. She was talented. She was good. That was painted in Paris.

RPQ: She's where a lot of the talent came from, I bet.
WEW: Yep. Yes, she took some prizes.

RPQ: I read that your father once discovered three medals after she died, that he never knew about. He was evidently looking through some of her possessions and discovered these medals which she'd won in Paris, and he never knew about it.
WEW: Yes, in Paris. Some of her paintings are here in the attic, too.

RPQ: This is the kind of work you find in a museum. Is this oil?
WEW: Yes.

RPQ: She lived to be very old, didn't she?
WEW: We were never quite sure how old she was.[11] She never would tell. She really outlived them all. [*Referring to some family photographs*] This is Dad here. Out here in the side yard in the spring, near the shadbush. He loved that. That's a native tree, but it's been neglected. Did you ever hear of the shadbush?

RPQ: No. On the other hand, I'm not familiar with....
WEW: Well, you know what a dogwood is, don't you? Dogwood, which has a rather dramatic display in the springtime, along the edge of the woods, well, the shadbush is the other white along the edge of the woods in springtime. And it has beautiful white flowers. Dad was a great champion of the shadbush. He said to his friend, Rudy Roehrs, over in East Rutherford, "You know, adopt this this thing, and make

people appreciate it! Sell it!" We have two beauties here on the property he bought in. Pulled them up by the roots up on the cliffs in West Paterson there, near Garret Mountain. So, that was one of his favorite things, local, native. And it was historically important to the American Indian. The shadbush is also known as a service berry, and they depended on it a great deal for food in the late spring, early summer. It's also great wood, used for tool handles, stuff like that.

RPQ: How do you feel about the construction of the William Carlos Williams Center?[12] *It is long overdue?*

WEW: Oh, I don't know. I think it's something the college wanted, and they're going after it. I think the community has been bulldozed into thinking that.... I don't know.

RPQ: It doesn't affect you one way or the other?

WEW: It doesn't affect me. I've contributed to it; I'm expected to. He was my father. But, I don't think it's a gut thing. It doesn't come from the grass roots or anything like that. I think a salesman at Fairleigh Dickinson got an idea, and the college will use the facility for its purposes, too. Ah, that's how I feel about it. Most of the red-hot enthusiasm in the community about the center is from the old-timers who are used to going there to the movies. They'd been going there to the movies since 1920. And they want to go to the movies, you know, forever. Yep. There are going to be three theaters, I think. You can go to the movies all day and night.

RPQ: I'm happy about it! The last time I heard, the movies are going to cost $1.50 each.

WEW: That's right. That's the nicest part.

RPQ: That's great. And you're going to have, like the Thalia in New York, the foreign films and the old Bogart movies, and they're gonna have another theater with maybe two or three month old "current films."

WEW: There's projected to be the home for the New Jersey Ballet and the New Jersey Symphony Orchestra.

RPQ: I didn't know that. I knew the ballet would go there.

RPQ: One thing my wife always says to me is that she wonders, she says, you know. Rich, you should warn people, especially at work, and so on, that anything which happens in your presence may become part of a poem. Which is true. And I write about anything. So, the question is, was it ever a problem for you to think that your personal life might become part of a body of literature?

WEW: Not in the least. Not in the least.

RPQ: Did it ever dawn on you that that was happening?

WEW: No, his sources never concerned me whatsoever. As you know, his writing was in his patients. This was where he got his inspiration. In his patients, in his practice. Without them he was bored. He had nothing to say. However, I was always surprised when poems came out with things about my three kids, poems about my ex-wife and my brother's ex-wife. I'm sure I'm in his work in many places where I'm not aware of it. I'm not concerned. It doesn't interest me. As I say, I'm not a scholar....

RPQ: Have you ever felt isolated, as your father, temperamentally from the community, or in any way more than the average?

WEW: I think by nature I'd be isolated no matter where I lived. When I lived in New York, when I lived in....

RPQ: Why is that?

WEW: I'm quite content to be where I am. I have a sort of self-sufficient little world of my own. I "do my thing." I'm not too dependent on other people; yet, I can relate easily with people. No problem. Maybe I learned it from him, I don't know. I have enough intellectual curiosity, enough intelligence, background, education, to be able to pick up a spy story, I can pick up a *National Geographic*, I can read excerpts from the Bible. What the hell, there's no reason for anybody to be lonely. I'm isolated but not a....

RPQ: No more than the average intelligent person is....

WEW: I love to get my hands in the dirt. I love to garden. I'm a lousy odd job guy. I painted this room. It was a labor of love. It was a lot of work, it really was. Sand it, spackle it, three coats on the ceiling, on the walls. But, Mimi wanted it done. I figured, gee, I'll save a couple of thousand bucks and do it ourselves. We picked out the colors and we did it. I like to do things like this, once in a while. I'm through with painting for a few months, I hope. I love to split wood, use the fireplace a lot. As I said, I'm a fisherman, a gardener. I'm very much interested in building walls, dry walls, not cement walls, fieldstone. Sure I'm isolated. I told my wife repeatedly, she comes to this community as a stranger, and she's found it....

RPQ: Where is your wife from?

WEW: From down the pike a bit here, Maplewood, originally from Connecticut. She was born up in Connecticut. Came here as a bride with her first husband. And it's been difficult for her because I am a pretty isolated guy and rather self-sufficient, and lot of my peer group are either dead or moved away.... Rutherford is a town that's changed tremendously. It's a deteriorating community. It's sad. And the guys and gals I went to school with are gone. I don't think I could pick a half dozen people in town who I went to school with. They're gone.

RPQ: You're saying it's part of the condition of actually aging. As you age, people move ....

WEW: They die. And lose interest, too. You know, they couldn't care less. I mean [laughs]. I have an illustration of it: my wife and I were down in New Orleans. I was down for a medical thing down there, and it struck me. A kid that I had the greatest admiration for, a little bit older than you are, and I thought—I'm gonna call this guy. He had an odd name. I looked in the directory, and sure enough, there he was. And I called him up. And I said, hey, this is Bill Williams. Remember me from Maine, 1923 or '4, something like that?

RPQ: How long ago did you make this call?

WEW: Oh, a couple of years ago. And he says, yeah, I remember you. You liked to fish. He'd been an avid fisherman too, this guy. Ah, I said, yeah, how are you? What are you up to? What are you doing? Anything to open him up. Ah, he wasn't interested. What are you kidding [a small laugh]. I said, oh sorry. And that was it. I was so titillated by the idea of calling this guy up and really surprising him, and maybe just saying just for auld lang syne and a few happy phrases, but aaaaach! No interest at all!

RPQ: Your dad talked about, he stayed in Rutherford, but he seemed to imply a certain resentment he had, a certain dissatisfaction that he never really resolved, with having stayed in Rutherford for all the obvious reasons—his family, his practice, his ties in that sense, but I guess if I could make a question out of it, it would be, it's kind of tied to the other question: have you had any, do you feel any of that dissatisfaction?

WEW: Stuck in the mud.

RPQ: What was his dissatisfaction with Rutherford?

WEW: I'm not sure that he was too dissatisfied with Rutherford, because he had a lot of friends here, and he was the kind of guy that, he was sought out. I mean, people came looking for him, you know, because of his role as a physician, because of his role as a writer. I mean, as far as Rutherford people, his dissatisfaction—not dissatisfaction—his disillusionment with Rutherford, after his reputation came through, in Rutherford nothing happened. [Laughs] Nothing! He'd get the national this award or that award, and people would say, "Did you write that?" [in a mocking tone] or another one would say, "Oh, you write all those funny poems. You know. Doc, what'ya mean when you write…." Everybody was always asking him, "What'ya mean, what'ya mean," and he'd say, "Look. Read it. If you like it, good. If it doesn't mean anything to you, forget it. Forget it. It means what it says." He wouldn't even explain it to us kids. Nothing.

RPQ: I touched on some of the problems you had with your dad, but can you think of a … can you single out maybe one or two of the fondest recollections you have of your father?

WEW: Of Dad?

RPQ: Yes, something you're really fond of.

WEW: Very difficult. I think probably some of the, uh, I, I often think of an incident where he and I—we both liked to garden—had that with him, we were working out in the garden, back of the house, pulling up weeds, turning over soil, clearing something for something, exactly what I don't know; but, at the time Jimmy Durante was a top comedian, and Dad really enjoyed Jimmy Durante, He thought his stuff was on the beam. That and Red, ah, somebody.

RPQ: Red Skelton.

WEW: Red Skelton was another comedian he liked. Well, anyway, we were pulling up weeds, and, ah, we pulled up, ah, God, a big clump of roots and soil, and everything came up with this thing. And he said, like Jimmy would say, "Ah, cha, cha, cha, what a root system, what a root system!" And he sent that to Jimmy Durante, and Jimmy wrote back: Dear Doc, Thanks for the gag, Jimmy. [laughs] So, we had moments, and I think in some of these poems, not poems, some of these articles I've written it'll reveal moments where we saw eye to eye in a reasonable father-son relationship. You know, I think he tried very hard. He tried to get out of character sometimes and get closer to us kids. He made a real effort. When we were little kids, he'd push us in a swing out here in the yard. Later on, at camp in Maine, he'd take us out and row us around the lake all afternoon so we could catch some fish, uh, but things of that kind. I don't, uh, nothing terrific, nothing outside of those physical, menial, little things that we had in common, because after all we didn't have a great meeting of minds except in medicine, which we shared. We could talk intelligently, we could correspond intelligently on medicine, on patients' symptoms, when Mom was sick, when my kids were sick, so we shared that.

RPQ: I remember a letter he wrote to you when you were a student at Williams. I find it really a very fascinating letter. It was in Thirlwall's collection.[13]

WEW: I just got those back.

RPQ: It was a good letter. It was a letter written from a father to a son, you, about.... You evidently had written him or were going through some problems, the normal confusions of being a sensitive young man in an academic world, and he was telling you, I remember one of those things he talked about, how athletes get everything they want when they're young; he talked about the benefits of the physical life, especially when you're young. He told you to hang in there, and when you're older you'd realize how important it is to have a good mind, good intelligence, good sensibility. There seemed to be a sincere closeness and affection between you two. I never received that kind of a letter from my father. I don't think he could have written that kind of a letter.

WEW: Well, my dad had that kind of a mind, that's all. It wasn't hard for him to write a letter like that. It was something at which he was a pro. He observed, studied. He was able to make that kind of diagnosis and prescription. This is the way it is today; this is the way it's going to be tomorrow because ... it's perfectly rational.

RPQ: And also another letter, I recall, written to you when you were in the service in the Pacific, and it was a kind of apologetic letter saying perhaps he had not been the best of fathers, but he apologized to you for having laughed at you as a boy....[14]

WEW: Oh yes that was at camp—when I'd lost a canoe race.

RPQ: Yes, you had cried as a young kid....

WEW: Yep, I was good at canoe paddling and somebody had cut me off.

RPQ: You still remember this.

WEW: I was really upset. I always won the fishing prize, but this year I was going to win the canoe race, too. Yep, and I guess what'ya tell your kid: "Ah, come on, it's just a canoe race," you know, forget it, but it was very important to me. Funny, those moments come back so vividly, like old men, those childhood things, they're right there, not lost at all.

RPQ: Have you ever felt a need to compete with your father?

WEW: Compete?

RPQ: Compete ... since he was a doctor. You're a doctor. Have you never felt, you know, I have to fill my father's shoes, that type of thing?

WEW: No. I think, if anything, I've played it down, put it out of my way, to be my own person, and I was resentful sometimes, too, at the hospital, because everything was put in my way.

RPQ: What do you mean, put in your way?

WEW: Made easy for me.

RPQ: Oh, I see.

WEW: Want to be head of the department? Want to be chief of the staff, want to be this, want to be that? And it was nice to work in an atmosphere where he was really, ah,....

RPQ: Admired.

WEW: Oh, God, worshipped. Some letters from nurses, I'm still delving and getting stuff. But, uh, this Paul Mariani, he's a fantastic detective. God, he digs! You're gotta read his book.

RPQ: It's coming out soon?

WEW: It's on the presses. He's turned up more stuff! He found these letters of mine at Yale—these letters that Thirlwall had. Thirlwall had'em, but he snuck'em out of there somehow. I'm sure, big hearted Dad, you know—"Auh, you wanna use these letters?" And then I never saw them again. And then Paul had an idea. He said, "You know, maybe we can get some of them." And, ah, Yale was never officially designated as the repository of all the William Carlos Williams material, whatever. But people had a tendency to feel that it was. If you had something about William Carlos Williams and you didn't know what to do with it, you sent it to Yale.

RPQ: And Buffalo too?

WEW: Buffalo, or course that was due to Charles Abbott.[15] They got a big load, and then it stopped. And then Yale came in here, physically came in with Dad's permission, and ransacked the place and hauled it all off.... So, ah, between the two places, everything is sent there. And Paul just had an idea. One night he was driving back from here to Amherst and it struck him as he was crossing the Tappan Zee Bridge that he should go to New Haven. So, he turned off at New Haven, stayed in a motel, and got into the library the next day. He talked to someone, and sure enough, there they were. And he said the same thing. He said, "Gee, you know, your dad had pretty warm friendships with some of the nurses over in Passaic," he said, "Any of them still around?" I gave him some names. He checked on them, and lo and behold, the stuff is beginning to flow now [laughs]. Letters, photocopies of letters that he wrote. These gals communicated with him when he was ill or something, and he wrote back.

RPQ: This will be in the book?

WEW: Oh, yes. Yep. Some of the letters are right there.

[*At this point, Dr. Williams rose, still talking about letters used in Paul Mariani's biography, and moved into another section of the house where his father's desk remains. The interview ended, officially, with the doctor sharing with me various items from his father, including letters and postcards written as far back as an early visit to Mexico with a dying patient, file card notes filled with young WCW's keen observations of birds, and the severely distorted script of the poet written after his strokes.*]

Chapter Notes

Preface

1. William Carlos Williams, "Foreword," *Autobiography of William Carlos Williams* (New Directions, 1958), np [1].

2. For details of the earliest scholarship on William Carlos Williams, see Paul Mariani, *The Poet and His Critics* (American Library Association, 1975), which covers scholarship published through 1973, and Joseph Brogunier, "An Annotated Bibliography of Works about William Carlos Williams: 1974–1982," in *William Carlos Williams: Man and Poet*, ed. Carroll F. Terrell (National Poetry Foundation, 1983), 453–586. In turn, these works build on the first book-length bibliography of Williams scholarship, namely Emily Mitchell Wallace, *A Bibliography of William Carlos Williams* (Wesleyan University Press, 1968).

3. The book that resulted was Ian D. Copestake, *The Ethics of William Carlos Williams's Poetry* (Camden House, 2010).

Introduction

1. William Carlos Williams, *The Collected Poems of William Carlos Williams, Volume I, 1909–1939*, ed. A. Walton Litz and Christopher MacGowan (New Directions, 1991), 183.

2. See Robert Coles and Thomas Roma, *House Calls with William Carlos Williams, MD* (powerHouse Books, 2008).

3. Williams, *Collected Poems*, Vol. I, 372.

4. Ann Fisher-Wirth, "The Allocations of Desire: 'This Is Just to Say' and Flossie Williams's 'Reply,'" *William Carlos Williams Review* 22.2. Special Issue: Williams and Psychoanalysis (Fall 1996), 47–56, offers an interpretation that investigates the poem's "darker implications" (49).

5. William Carlos Williams, *The Collected Poems of William Carlos Williams, Volume II, 1939–1962*, ed. Christopher MacGowan (New Directions, 1991), 317–18.

Author's Note: Closer to the Grain

1. Four biographies published by 1995 include Reed Whittemore, *William Carlos Williams: Poet from Jersey* (1975); Linda Welshimer Wagner, ed., *Interviews with William Carlos Williams* (1976); Paul Mariani, *William Carlos Williams: A New World Naked* (1981); Neil Baldwin, *To All Gentleness: William Carlos Williams, the Doctor Poet* (1984). Subsequent biographies include Herbert Leibowitz, *"Something Urgent I Have to Say to You": The Life and Works of William Carlos Williams* (2011).

2. The novels of the Stecher family trilogy are *White Mule* (1937); *In the Money* (1940); and *The Build-Up* (1952). Prose collections including the medical stories include *Life Along the Passaic River* (1938); *Make Light of It: Collected Stories of William Carlos Williams* (1950); and *The Doctor Stories*, comp. Robert Coles (1984).

3. Williams, *Autobiography*, 174.

Chapter Notes

Chapter 1

1. Quoted from a letter to William Eric from Fred Bunker, former Rutherford Borough historian, dated July 7, 1988.
2. Williams, *Autobiography*, 3.
3. Williams, *Autobiography*, 20.
4. Williams, *Autobiography*, 29.
5. Williams, *Autobiography*, 29.
6. Williams, *Autobiography*, 29.
7. Williams, *Collected Poems*, Vol. I, 167.
8. Williams, *Collected Poems*, Vol. II, 58.
9. Williams, *Collected Poems*, Vol. I, 323.
10. Williams, *Collected Poems*, Vol. I, 457.
11. Williams, *Collected Poems*, Vol. I, 267.
12. Williams, *Collected Poems*, Vol. I, 92.
13. Williams, *Collected Poems*, Vol. I, 348

Chapter 2

1. A version of this chapter was first published in the *William Carlos Williams Newsletter* 5.1 (Spring 1979): 1–5. This material is used by permission of The Pennsylvania State University Press.
2. "This Is Just to Say" (1934) in Williams, *Collected Poems*, Vol. I, 372.
3. Charles Demuth, *Lady Slippers* or *Pink Lady Slippers* (1918). Transparent watercolor over graphite on wove paper. Dimensions: 18 x 11 7/8 in. (45.7 x 30.1 cm). Housed in the Munson Williams, Utica, New York. https://munsonwilliams.emuseum.com/objects/11635/lady-slippers.
4. Captain Red Ruud is mentioned in Mariani's biography of Williams in relation to a 1950 catalog note Williams had written for an exhibition of seven portraits of French photographer and painter Dora Maar by Pablo Picasso. Mariani reflects that while writing this note, Williams "may have stopped to look up at the death mask a seaman admirer of his, Red Ruud, had brought back from Malaya and which held such a prominent place in the living room, the lidless eyes staring out on the void" (597).
5. Demuth's *End of the Parade—Coatesville, Pa.* (1920). Private collection of the Williams estate.
6. *Children's Games* by Flemish Renaissance artist Pieter Brueghel the Elder. Oil-on-panel, painted in 1560. Kunsthistorisches Museum, Vienna. https://www.khm.at/en/artworks/children-s-games-321.
7. Eyvind Earle's "View Under the Bridge," "depicting the construction of New York City from a view under the bridges of Manhattan. The restored painting has been placed on permanent loan to the World Trade Center by the granddaughter of William Carlos Williams. The poet commissioned the painting in 1943" (https://www.antiquesandthearts.com/rarely-seen-eyvind-earle-work-to-honor-one-world-trade/).
8. "Poem (As the cat)" (1930), in Williams, *Collected Poems*, Vol. I, 352.

Chapter 3

1. A version of this chapter first appeared as part of Eric Williams's "Foreword" to the 1982 New Directions edition of William Carlos Williams's 1959 memoir of his mother, *Yes, Mrs. Williams: A Personal Record of My Mother* (McDowell, Obolensky, 1959), ix–xvi.
2. Williams, *Yes, Mrs. Williams*, 51.
3. Williams, *Autobiography*, 110.
4. Edith Heal, "FURTHER CONVERSATIONS WITH FLOSSIE," *William Carlos Williams Newsletter* 3.1 (Spring 1977): 1–7, 1. Lucy (Lucille Russ [later Wooten]) was the longest serving of the Williams's maids, who worked for the family for at least 40 years from the first decade of the twentieth century.

Chapter 4

1. "Greasy Grind" illustrated postcard in the Williams family archive. Text on the right reads: "Greasy Grind! Was ist los? Write a fellow! Ed." As Paul Mariani explains it in his biography of Williams, "[t]he two Williamses families would grow up side by side in Rutherford: Ed in his parents' home at 131 West Passaic; and Bill at 9 Ridge Road. [...] But really the two families belonged to different worlds with different values" (112).

2. It is likely that this work was Williams's 1923 volume of prose-poetry *Spring and All*.

3. For a comprehensive edition of 200 early letters sent by William Carlos to Edgar and housed at the University of Pennsylvania's Rare Book and Manuscript Library, see Andrew Krivak, ed., *The Letters of William Carlos Williams to Edgar Irving Williams, 1902–1912* (Fairleigh Dickinson University Press, 2009).

4. Krivak, ed., *Letters*, 37.

Chapter 5

1. The "A&P" (Great Atlantic & Pacific Tea Company) refers to an iconic chain of American grocery stores that operated from 1859 to 2015.

2. Letter and sketch in the Yale Collection of American Literature archive.

3. Williams, *Autobiography*, 128.

4. See also Williams's 1921 poem "Peter Kipp to the High School" concerning the civic dispute over the fate and use of Kipp's land after his death in 1920 in Williams, *Collected Poems*, Vol. I, 566–7.

5. This statement was first incorporated into Williams's poetry as a line in his 1927 poem "Paterson," parts of which were then included in Book One (1946) of his long poem *Paterson*. For the early poem, see Williams, *Collected Poems*, Vol. I, 263.

6. For a reflection on the importance of the science of walking to Williams's writing, see T. Hugh Crawford, "Walking with William Carlos Williams," *William Carlos Williams Review* 34.2 (2017): 93–109.

7. See Williams, *Autobiography*, 123.

8. Williams, *Collected Poems*, Vol. II, 423–24.

9. A stone marker (the Daniel Webster marker) was erected at this spot by the Stratton Mountain Club on August 10, 1915, which reads: "This rock marks the spot where Daniel Webster spoke to about 15000 people at Whig Convention July 7 & 8, 1840." https://dp.la/item/c63cd0a0714b0903a125d1b76d44bc90.

10. William Bird was an American editor who ran Three Mountains Press in Paris and published Williams's *The Great American Novel* in 1923. On a trip to Europe from January 1924, Williams recounted meeting Bill for the first time (having on the same day met Constantin Brâncuși and before an evening spent with James and Nora Joyce): "Bill was a tall, sharp-bearded American businessman who looked as though he had been mellowed in Chambertine, gentle, kindly and informal. I fell for him instantly" (Williams, *Autobiography*, 189).

Chapter 6

1. Williams reflects on this incident, commenting that "[i]t certainly altered my life" (83), in the "French Hospital" chapter of his *Autobiography*, 76–85.

2. Williams, *Autobiography*, 106.

3. Williams, *Autobiography*, 106.

4. Of this first published volume of his poems, titled simply *Poems* (1909), the editors of the first volume of *Collected Poems* explain that Williams "explicitly told his publisher James Laughlin that these poems were not to be reprinted and we have followed his wish [...]" (Williams, *Collected Poems*, Vol. I, xviii). Williams reflects on this publication of "bad Keats" in his *Autobiography*, 106–08.

5. Williams, *Autobiography*, 108.

6. Williams, *Autobiography*, 109.

7. Williams, *Autobiography*, 111.

8. Sartorius's translations include *Kore in der Hölle: Frühe Schriften* (Berlin: Carl Hanser, 1988).

9. A diptheria epidemic provides the historical context for Williams's 1938 short story "The Use of Force" and is the backdrop for the dramatic and violent examination of the throat of the child patient, Mathilda, suspected of having contracted the disease.

10. On the role of Sir Alexander Fleming in "discovering" penicillin, essentially by accident, in 1928, see https://www.nobelprize.org/prizes/medicine/1945/fleming/biographical/.

11. Williams, *A Voyage to Pagany* (Macaulay, 1928), 148.

12. Williams, *A Voyage to Pagany,* 148–49.

13. Williams, *A Voyage to Pagany,* 152.

14. Krivak, ed., *Letters,* 199.

15. Krivak, ed., *Letters,* 202.

16. Williams's account of this meeting and subsequent events is given in his *Autobiography,* 118–19.

17. Williams, *Autobiography,* 120.

18. Williams, *Autobiography,* 120.

19. See Williams, *Autobiography* 121–24.

20. Williams, *Autobiography,* 92.

21. Krivak, ed., *Letters,* 218.

22. Krivak, ed., *Letters,* 225.

Chapter 7

1. A version of this chapter was first published in the *William Carlos Williams Review* 8.1 (Spring 1982): 1–7. This material is used by permission of The Pennsylvania State University Press.

2. Williams, *Collected Poems,* Vol. I, 92.

3. The photo, taken by Elliott Erwitt, can, for instance, be seen in Neda M. Westlake, "The William Carlos Williams Collection at the University of Pennsylvania," *William Carlos Williams Newsletter* 4.1 (Spring 1978): 23–25, 25, though the caption given for the full-page photo incorrectly states that the building Williams is walking out of is the "Unitarian Church on Park Avenue" (25). The building is the Rutherford Free Library which until 1895 was the First Presbyterian Church. It was demolished and a new town library was built on the same location in 1958 designed by William Carlos's brother Edgar.

Chapter 8

1. A version of this chapter was first published in the *William Carlos Williams Newsletter* 5.2 (Fall 1979): 1–4. This material is used by permission of The Pennsylvania State University Press.

2. As a popular English essayist and poet, Lamb (1775–1883) famously featured food and its consumption in his works, such as in his essay "A Dissertation on Roast Pig" or his poem "Orange."

Chapter 9

1. A version of this chapter was originally published in the *William Carlos Williams Newsletter* 3.2 (Fall 1977): 1–5. This material is used by permission of The Pennsylvania State University Press.

2. An exploration of Williams's relationship to automobiles in his life and writing can be found in Joel Duncan, "'Rolls Rough': William Carlos Williams on the Thrills and Ills of Automobility," *Modernism/modernity* 29.3 (September 2022): 543–71.

3. On Williams's own active involvement in the local county mosquito commission, see Paul Cappucci, "Driving Through the Fog of Modernity: Mosquito Extermination, Progress, and *The Great American Novel,*" *William Carlos Williams Review* 42.1 (2025): 1–19.

Chapter 10

1. Some parts of this chapter were originally published in William Eric Williams, "The Physical," *William Carlos Williams Review* 8.1 (Spring 1982): 1–7.

This material is used by permission of The Pennsylvania State University Press.

2. This expression of frustration at a pitcher issuing a walk became the popular commentator's catchphrase.

3. Krivak, ed., *Letters*, 268.

4. Krivak, ed., *Letters*, 301.

5. Krivak, ed., *Letters*, 302.

6. In 1932, when William Eric was 18 years old, he had an essay titled "On Catching a Trout" published in *The Rutherfordian*, the literary magazine of Rutherford High School.

Chapter 11

1. Charles Abbott founded the Poetry Collection of the University of Buffalo Lockwood Library in 1935 where he was director and where, at Abbott's suggestion, Williams was at this time "beginning to deposit large amounts of his manuscripts and letters" (Paul Mariani, *William Carlos Williams: A New World Naked*, [McGraw-Hill, 1981], 435).

2. On Williams's association with Gratwick farm, see Emily Mitchell Wallace, "Musing in the Highlands and Valleys: The Poetry of Gratwick Farm," *William Carlos Williams Review* 8.1 (Spring 1982): 8–41.

3. Williams, *Collected Poems*, Vol. II, 102–03. On the poem's publication background and its relationship to the sculpture of William Gratwick, see Christopher MacGowan's notes in Williams, *Collected Poems*, Vol. II, 467.

Chapter 12

1. Williams, "Foreword," *Autobiography*, np [1].

2. Williams, *Autobiography*, 3.

3. See Williams, *Autobiography*, 12.

4. On the Williamses' personal and historical family association with Unitarianism in Rutherford, see Ian D. Copestake, *The Ethics of William Carlos Williams's Poetry* (Camden House, 2010), 6–24; 29–34; 56–64.

5. Williams, *Autobiography*, 48.

6. Williams, *Autobiography*, 67–68.

7. Hilda Doolittle, *Tribute to Freud* (New Directions, 1956), 107.

8. Krivak, ed., *Letters*, 75.

9. Krivak, ed., *Letters*, 75–76.

10. Krivak, ed., *Letters*, 112.

11. Williams, *Autobiography*, 69.

12. Williams, *Autobiography*, 70.

13. Hugh Witemeyer, ed., *Pound/Williams: Selected Letters of Ezra Pound and William Carlos Williams* (New Directions, 1996), 13.

14. Williams, *Autobiography*, 90.

15. Williams, *Autobiography*, 176.

16. Williams, *Autobiography*, 177.

17. Williams, *Autobiography*, 219.

18. Krivak, ed., *Letters*, 118.

19. In July 1943, Pound was indicted by the U.S. government as a traitor for his supposed support of Mussolini via radio broadcasts from his base in Italy from 1942. He was granted psychiatric treatment to determine his mental fitness to stand trial, and "on 1 January 1946 was moved to Howard Hall for the criminally insane at St. Elizabeths Hospital" (Alec Marsh, *Ezra Pound* [Reaktion Books, 2011], 171). Deemed unfit to face a trial, Pound remained confined at St. Elizabeths until 1958.

20. John C. Thirlwall, ed., *The Selected Letters of William Carlos Williams* (New Directions, 1957), 20–1.

21. Williams, *Autobiography*, 164.

22. Williams, *Autobiography*, 168.

23. Williams, *Autobiography*, 168.

24. Williams, *Autobiography*, 169.

25. Williams, *Autobiography*, 169.

26. Williams, *Autobiography*, 169.

27. Williams, *Autobiography*, 169.

28. Williams, *Autobiography*, 164.

29. See Williams, *Autobiography*, 101.

30. Clinicopathological conferences, or CPCs, were initially informal patient discussions, before taking on a structured format where a clinician would analyze a patient's history before developing a diagnosis. This would then be confirmed by the pathology findings. They were introduced into the U.S. in the

early twentieth century through their use at Harvard Medical School.

31. A photo by Eve Arnold of Anne Oley at work with Williams overseeing a premature baby in an incubator was published in *Coronet* 42 (October 1957): 42–51. It was part of a feature article by Gerald Frank on Williams titled "A Rich, a Full Life." See William Eric's discussion of this incident in his interview in this book with Richard P. Quatrone.

32. Helen Williamson Hall was a patient of William Carlos Williams and was interviewed about the poet-doctor by her son, James Edward Hall, on May 8, 1977, for the department of Oral Research History, Columbia University.

33. The club was established in 1916 "by ten Rutherford couples, including Dr. and Mrs. Williams, as well as Mr. and Mrs. Edgar Williams," to provide an "irreverent" platform for discussion across a range of topics "of human interest" (John G. Dollar, "William Carlos Williams and the Polytopic Club," in *William Carlos Williams: Man and Poet*, 93–106, 94).

34. Witemeyer, ed., *Pound/Williams*, 279.

35. Musical terms for "moderately slow tempo without energy" and "to be performed in a lively manner."

Chapter 13

1. See the third volume of William Carlos Williams's Stecher trilogy of novels, *The Build-Up* (1952), 317–18, and also references in Mariani, *A New World Naked*, 111–12.

2. Williams, *Collected Poems*, Vol. I, 74–76.

3. A variation of the Scandinavian card game *Fem-kort* (Danish for "Five Cards").

4. Harris was an Irish-born editor and novelist "who became an American citizen in April 1921. In 1922, he travelled to Berlin to publish his best-known work, his autobiography *My Life and Loves* (published in four volumes, 1922–1927). It is notorious for its graphic descriptions of Harris' purported sexual encounters and for its exaggeration of the scope of his adventures and his role in history" (https://en.wikipedia.org/wiki/Frank_Harris).

5. From William Wordsworth's 1798 poem "The Tables Turned" which was published as part of the poet's *Lyrical Ballads*.

6. Williams had first encountered Laughlin, heir of the Jones & Laughlin Steel Corporation of Pittsburgh, in 1934, when he responded to a call for written contributions to the *Harvard Advocate* which Laughlin worked on as an undergraduate at Harvard (see Mariani, *A New World Naked*, 352). In 1936, Laughlin established the New Directions publishing house for whom Williams would become a cornerstone author. Their first meeting took place the previous year at 9 Ridge Road and is described in Ian S. MacNiven, *"Literchoor Is My Beat": A Life of James Laughlin, Publisher of New Directions* (Farrar, Straus and Giroux, 2014), 88–89.

7. See the next chapter, "The Doctor."

8. What became known as the "Day of Infamy" speech was delivered by Franklin D. Roosevelt to a joint session of Congress on December 8, 1941, the day after the attack on the United States Pacific Fleet moored at Pearl Harbor on Oahu, Hawaii.

9. From the Lord's Prayer, specifically the concluding doxology in Matthew 6:13.

10. For more details about this correspondence, see Theodora Rapp Graham, "'As if you had never known me': William Carlos Williams's Letters to William Eric in the Pacific Theater, World War Two," *William Carlos Williams Review* 36.2 (2019): 53–63.

Chapter 14

1. A version of this chapter was originally published in *William Carlos*

Williams Review 9.1/2, Centennial Issue (Fall 1983): 35–42. This material is used by permission of The Pennsylvania State University Press.

2. In the chapter of his *Autobiography* covering this period, "First Years of Practice," Williams says his "first case was one of dandruff" (127).

3. A version of this section of the chapter was originally published in William Eric Williams, "The School Physician's Notebook: A Cameo of William Carlos Williams," *Literature and Medicine* 2 (1983): 3–8.

4. In 1983, Emily Mitchell Wallace with the help of William Eric Williams published an article containing exact-size facsimiles and transcriptions of the entire contents of this notebook. See Emily Mitchell Wallace, "The Little Red Notebook of William Carlos Williams," *William Carlos Williams Review* 9.1/2, Centennial Issue (1983): 1–34.

5. For more details of Williams's work on the Commission, see Paul Cappucci, "Driving Through the Fog of Modernity: Mosquito Extermination, Progress, and *The Great American Novel*," *William Carlos Williams Review* 42.1 (2025): 1–19.

6. Sir William Osler (1849–1919) was a Canadian physician, Regius Professor of Medicine at the University of Oxford, and one of the four founding professors of Johns Hopkins Hospital in the U.S. where he established the first residency program for the specialty training of physicians.

7. This health scare was reported in the following article on the front page of *The New York Times*: "YOUNG ROOSEVELT SAVED BY NEW DRUG; Doctor Used Prontylin in Fight on Streptococcus Infection of the Throat. CONDITION ONCE SERIOUS But Youth, in Boston Hospital, Gains Steadily—Fiancee, Reassured, Leaves Bedside," *The New York Times* (December 17, 1936): 1.

8. A formal, written notice sent to a customer or client who has an overdue payment.

Chapter 15

1. A version of this chapter was first published in the *William Carlos Williams Review* 9.1/2, Centennial Issue (Fall 1983): 42–44. This material is used by permission of The Pennsylvania State University Press.

2. The Buffalo nickel or Indian Head nickel is a copper-nickel five-cent piece struck by the United States Mint from 1913 to 1938.

3. Veblen's theory was first outlined in his 1899 book *The Theory of the Leisure Class: An Economic Study of Institutions.*

4. Witemeyer, ed., *Pound/Williams* 95. The article by Pound that Williams praises was "Dr. Williams' Position," *The Dial* 85.5 (November 1928): 395–404.

Chapter 16

1. This reaction to, and description of, Flossie being born appears verbatim in the opening pages of William Carlos Williams's 1937 novel *White Mule* (9–14, 11), the first of his Stecher family trilogy of novels.

2. See the chapter "Medical Education in Leipzig, 1909–1910."

3. *The Dog & the Fever: A Perambulatory Novella*, by Francisco de Quevedo who published under the name of Pedro Espinosa, translated by William Carlos Williams and Raquel Hélène Williams (Shoe String Press, 1954). According to Jonathan Cohen in his introduction to a 2018 edition of the translation, "in the fall of 1936, a few months after the start of the Spanish Civil War that deeply roused [Williams's] personal Spanish identity, he set about to bring this novella into English with the help of his mother" ("Introduction. William Carlos Williams and His Clever Dog: *Conceptismo* with a New Jersey Twist," *The Dog & the Fever: A Perambulatory Novella*, by Pedro Espinosa, translated by William Carlos Williams, Raquel Hélène Williams, edited by Jonathan Cohen [Wesleyan University Press, 2018], xiv).

4. On the tragic deaths of Floss's 14-year-old brother, Paul, and, later, her father, see Williams, *Autobiography*, 156 and 274.

5. Winfield Townley Scott and Williams had corresponded since the early 1940s, after Williams contributed poetry to the "New Verse" column Scott wrote for the *Providence Sunday Journal*. They first met in person in New York in 1950 before Scott moved to Santa Fe in 1954.

6. A colleague of Scott's at the *Providence Journal* from 1947, Ben Bagdikian went on to become a Pulitzer Prize–winning journalist and author of the acclaimed 1983 work *The Media Monopoly*.

7. Williams, *Collected Poems*, Vol. II, 437. This poem closes Williams's last book of poetry, *Pictures from Brueghel* (1962).

Chapter 17

1. In a letter to Ezra Pound on January 6, 1927, he reflects on the lack of money earned from his literary endeavors preventing him from giving up his medical practice, despite some recent successes, such as the *Dial* award he won the previous year and the money that contributed. He had also, however, lost $5,000 in an out-of-court settlement following a lawsuit brought against him relating to his short story "The Five-Dollar Guy" about a real-life seduction incident. However, the story was published without the names of the protagonists being changed (see Mariani, *A New World Naked*, 254–55). To Pound he writes: "Work now obsesses me—I mean my practice of medicine. The day is spent in sallys [*sic*] and retreats. The work pays. Had I the 'five grand' again, plus the Dial's two, plus what I could get for my house I could live on the income (modestly) for the balance of my days. But would I do it? I believe not—not yet; perhaps it would be cutting my own throat to cut off this fury of running around from house to house that somehow fires me with energy even while it exhausts me" (Witemeyer, ed., *Pound/Williams*, 79).

2. William Carlos Williams, *Paterson* (New Directions, 1995), 114.

3. From Williams's 1954 poem "For Eleanor and Bill Monahan," in *Collected Poems*, Vol. II, 255.

4. In addition to the incident William Eric relates in the "Dear Bo" chapter, several issues over the years saw Edgar distance himself from his brother. For instance, Mariani highlights how, since the early 1920s, "Ed had never forgiven him for making [the family's] Jewishness public. Ed had never believed it anyway, nor had many of his relatives" (Mariani, *A New World Naked*, 411).

5. Williams, *Autobiography*, 15.

Appendix

1. Essays published by William Eric Williams in the *William Carlos Williams Newsletter* from 1977 through to 1983, including early versions of chapters extended here: "Cars" (1977), "Food" (1979), "The House" (1979), "The Physical" (1982), "Money" (1983) and "The Doctor" (1983).

2. This is Theodora Rapp Graham, founding editor of the *William Carlos Williams Newsletter* in 1975, published by Penn State University Press, and which subsequently became the *William Carlos Williams Review*.

3. Williams co-edited this magazine with its founder Robert McAlmon. It ran for four issues between December 1920 and summer 1921, with a fifth issue appearing in June 1923.

4. Reed Whittemore, *William Carlos Williams: Poet from Jersey* (Houghton Mifflin, 1975), 239.

5. Shortly before this interview a local group of poets called the Passaic City Poets held a reading at 131 West Passaic Avenue in the house where William Carlos Williams and his brother Edgar grew up.

6. The interview was conducted a year before Paul Mariani's biography (*William Carlos Williams: A New World Naked*) came out and which William Eric had been helping Mariani with up to this point. The address of the house William Carlos Williams was born in was 115 West Passaic Avenue. The TV production mentioned here might be "In the American Grain," part of the *Eye on New York* series broadcast by CBS, aired in 1964, and directed by Albert Walker. More information on the film is provided by Chris MacGowan's note in *The Letters of Denise Levertov and William Carlos Williams*, ed. Chris MacGowan (New Directions, 1998), 126. With thanks to Chris MacGowan for his assistance.

7. Emily Mitchell Wallace. She was author of *A Bibliography of William Carlos Williams* (1968).

8. Williams, *Autobiography*, np [2].

9. This phrase and variants of it appear several times in Williams's long poem *Paterson* (pages 6, 9, 27, and 173) but was first used in a shorter poem of the same name, "Paterson," written in 1927 (see Williams, *Collected Poems*, vol. I, 263).

10. The term "beanball" comes from the early twentieth-century slang term "bean" for "head," and the phrase refers to a deliberate throw at the batter's head. Such a pitch is a serious offense and can lead to ejections and suspensions.

11. Raquel Hélène Rose Hoheb Williams lived to be 102.

12. The William Carlos Williams Center for the Performing Arts was opened in 1982, is located in downtown Rutherford, New Jersey, and was built on the site of a former movie house, the Rivoli Theater. Further information on the history of the Center can be found here: https://en.wikipedia.org/wiki/The_Williams_Center_(theater).

13. Letter to William Eric Williams dated March 13, 1935, in Thirlwall, ed., *Selected Letters*, 153–55.

14. Letter to William Eric Williams dated September 25, 1942, in Thirlwall, ed., *Selected Letters*, 201–03.

15. See the reference to Charles Abbott in the "Gardening" chapter above.

Bibliography

Brogunier, Joseph. "An Annotated Bibliography of Works about William Carlos Williams: 1974–1982." In *William Carlos Williams: Man and Poet.* Edited by Carroll F. Terrell, 453–586. National Poetry Foundation, 1983.

Cappucci, Paul. "Driving Through the Fog of Modernity: Mosquito Extermination, Progress, and *The Great American Novel.*" *William Carlos Williams Review* 42.1 (2025): 1–19.

Cohen, Jonathan. "Introduction. William Carlos Williams and His Clever Dog: *Conceptismo* with a New Jersey Twist." In *The Dog & the Fever: A Perambulatory Novella,* by Pedro Espinosa. Translated by William Carlos Williams and Raquel Hélène Williams. Edited by Jonathan Cohen. Wesleyan University Press, 2018.

Coles, Robert, and Thomas Roma. *House Calls with William Carlos Williams, MD.* powerHouse Books, 2008.

Copestake, Ian D. *The Ethics of William Carlos Williams's Poetry.* Camden House, 2010.

Crawford, T. Hugh. "Walking with William Carlos Williams." *William Carlos Williams Review* 34.2 (2017): 93–109.

Dollar, John G. "William Carlos Williams and the Polytopic Club." In *William Carlos Williams: Man and Poet.* Edited by Carroll F. Terrell, 93–106. National Poetry Foundation, 1983.

Doolittle, Hilda. *Tribute to Freud.* New Directions, 1956.

Duncan, Joel. "'Rolls Rough': William Carlos Williams on the Thrills and Ills of Automobility." *Modernism/modernity* 29.3 (September 2022): 543–71.

Espinosa, Pedro. *The Dog & the Fever: A Perambulatory Novella,* by Francisco de Quevedo who published under the name of Pedro Espinosa. Translated by William Carlos Williams and Raquel Hélène Williams. Shoe String Press, 1954.

Fisher-Wirth, Ann. "The Allocations of Desire: 'This Is Just to Say' and Flossie Williams's 'Reply.'" *William Carlos Williams Review* 22.2. Special Issue: Williams and Psychoanalysis (Fall 1996): 47–56.

Frank, Gerald. "A Rich, a Full Life." *Coronet* 42 (October 1957): 42–51.

Graham, Theodora Rapp. "'As if you had never known me': William Carlos Williams's Letters to William Eric in the Pacific Theater, World War Two." *William Carlos Williams Review* 36.2 (2019): 53–63.

Heal, Edith. "FURTHER CONVERSATIONS WITH FLOSSIE." *William Carlos Williams Newsletter* 3.1 (Spring 1977): 1–7.

Krivak, Andrew J., ed. *The Letters of William Carlos Williams to Edgar Irving Williams, 1902–1912.* Fairleigh Dickinson University Press, 2009.

MacGowan, Christopher, ed. *The Letters of Denise Levertov and William Carlos Williams.* New Directions, 1998.

MacNiven, Ian S. *"Literchoor Is My Beat": A Life of James Laughlin, Publisher of New Directions.* Farrar, Straus and Giroux, 2014.

Bibliography

Mariani, Paul. *The Poet and His Critics.* American Library Association, 1975.

Mariani, Paul. *William Carlos Williams: A New World Naked.* McGraw-Hill, 1981.

Marsh, Alec. *Ezra Pound.* Reaktion Books, 2011.

The New York Times. "YOUNG ROOSEVELT SAVED BY NEW DRUG; Doctor Used Prontylin in Fight on Streptococcus Infection of the Throat. CONDITION ONCE SERIOUS But Youth, in Boston Hospital, Gains Steadily—Fiancee, Reassured, Leaves Bedside." December 17, 1936: 1.

Pound, Ezra. "Dr. Williams' Position." *The Dial* 85.5 (November 1928): 395–404.

Thirlwall, John C., ed. *The Selected Letters of William Carlos Williams.* New Directions, 1957.

Wallace, Emily Mitchell. *A Bibliography of William Carlos Williams.* Wesleyan University Press, 1968.

Wallace, Emily Mitchell. "The Little Red Notebook of William Carlos Williams." *William Carlos Williams Review* 9.1/2. Centennial Issue (Fall 1983): 1–34.

Wallace, Emily Mitchell. "Musing in the Highlands and Valleys: The Poetry of Gratwick Farm." *William Carlos Williams Review* 8.1 (Spring 1982): 8–41.

Westlake, Neda M. "The William Carlos Williams Collection at the University of Pennsylvania." *William Carlos Williams Newsletter* 4.1 (Spring 1978): 23–25.

Whittemore, Reed. *William Carlos Williams: Poet from Jersey.* Houghton Mifflin, 1975.

Williams, William Carlos. *The Autobiography of William Carlos Williams.* New Directions, 1958.

Williams, William Carlos. *The Build-Up.* Random House, 1952.

Williams, William Carlos. *The Collected Poems of William Carlos Williams: Volume I, 1909–1939.* Edited by A. Walton Litz and Christopher MacGowan. New Directions, 1991.

Williams, William Carlos. *The Collected Poems of William Carlos Williams: Volume II, 1939–1962.* Edited by Christopher MacGowan. New Directions, 1991.

Williams, William Carlos. *Kore in der Hölle: Frühe Schriften.* Translated by Joachim Sartorius. Carl Hanser, 1988.

Williams, William Carlos. *Paterson.* New Directions, 1995.

Williams, William Carlos. *A Voyage to Pagany.* Macaulay, 1928.

Williams, William Carlos. *White Mule.* New Directions, 1937.

Williams, William Carlos. *Yes, Mrs. Williams: A Personal Record of My Mother.* McDowell, Obolensky, 1959.

Williams, William Eric. "Cars." *William Carlos Williams Newsletter* 3.2 (Fall 1977): 1–5.

Williams, William Eric. "The Doctor." *William Carlos Williams Review* 9.1/2. Centennial Issue (Fall 1983): 35–42.

Williams, William Eric. "Food." *William Carlos Williams Newsletter* 5.2 (Fall 1979): 1-4.

Williams, William Eric. "Foreword." In *Yes, Mrs. Williams: A Personal Record of My Mother.* New Directions, 1982.

Williams, William Eric. "The House." *William Carlos Williams Newsletter* 5.1 (Spring 1979): 1–5.

Williams, William Eric. "Money." *William Carlos Williams Review* 9.1/2. Centennial Issue (Fall 1983): 42–4.

Williams, William Eric. "On Catching a Trout." *The Rutherfordian* (1932).

Williams, William Eric. "The Physical." *William Carlos Williams Review* 8.1 (Spring 1982): 1–7.

Williams, William Eric. "The School Physician's Notebook: A Cameo of William Carlos Williams." *Literature and Medicine* 2 (1983): 3–8.

Witemeyer, Hugh, ed. *Pound/Williams: Selected Letters of Ezra Pound and William Carlos Williams.* New Directions, 1996.

Index

www.ingramcontent.com/pod-product-compliance
Lightning Source LLC
LaVergne TN
LVHW051621071026
849713LV00030B/387

* 9 7 8 1 4 7 6 6 9 9 5 5 4 *